Listening B2

Six practice tests for the
Cambridge B2 First

Jane Turner

PROSPERITY EDUCATION
www.prosperityeducation.net

Registered offices: Sherlock Close, Cambridge
CB3 0HP, United Kingdom

© Prosperity Education Ltd. 2022

First published 2022 | updated November 2022

ISBN: 978-1-913825-60-7

This publication is in copyright. Subject to statutory exception and to the provisions of relevant collective licensing agreements, no reproduction of any part may take place without the written permission of Prosperity Education.

'Cambridge B2 First' and 'FCE' are brands belonging to The Chancellor, Masters and Scholars of the University of Cambridge and are not associated with Prosperity Education or its products.

Audio production by FFG Media: www.ffgmedia.co.uk
Actors: Kirsty Gosnay; Rob Holman; Natalie Holman; Sandy Murray; Tom O'Reilly; Jane Turner; and David and Annie Pickering Pick.

The moral rights of the author have been asserted in accordance with the Copyright, Designs and Patents Act 1988.

For further information and resources, visit: www.prosperityeducation.net

To infinity and beyond.

Contents

Introduction	2
About the B2 First Listening	3
Test 1	5
Test 2	15
Test 3	25
Test 4	35
Test 5	45
Test 6	55
Answer keys	65
Transcript – Test 1	74
Transcript – Test 2	79
Transcript – Test 3	84
Transcript – Test 4	89
Transcript – Test 5	95
Transcript – Test 6	100
How to download the audio	106

Introduction

Welcome to this edition of sample tests for the Cambridge B2 First Listening, which has been written to replicate the Cambridge exam experience and has undergone rigorous expert and peer review. It comprises six B2 First Listening tests, 180 individual assessments with answer keys, audio transcripts, write-in answer sheets and a marking scheme, providing a large bank of high-quality, test-practice material for candidates.

The accompanying audio files to this resource are available to download from the Prosperity Education website (see the end of this book for instructions).

You or your students, if you are a teacher, will hopefully enjoy the wide range of recordings and benefit from the repetitive practice, something that is key to preparing for this part of the B2 First (FCE) examination.

I hope that you will find this resource a useful study aid, and I wish you all the best in preparing for the exam.

Jane Turner
Cambridge, 2022

Jane Turner is an associate lecturer in EAP/EFL at Anglia Ruskin University, Cambridge, and an EFL materials writer for international exam boards, universities and publishers. She previously worked as a Cambridge ESOL examiner for the British Council, and holds an MA in Educational Management and Cambridge CELTA and DELTA.

About the B2 First Listening

The Cambridge English B2 First (FCE) examination is a timed assessment, with approximately 40 minutes assigned to the Listening section, which is worth 20% of the available grade and comprises 30 individual assessments.

The Listening section of the examination tests candidates' abilities to follow a diverse range of spoken English, and to understand the speakers' personal opinions and attitudes, specific information being conveyed and also general meaning of lengthier monologues. It is broken down in to four parts with one mark awarded to each correct answer:

- Part 1 contains eight short recordings of individuals speaking in eight different situations. Each recording is followed by a multiple-choice question.

- Part 2 is a longer recording of an individual speaking about a specific topic. In each of the ten sentences that follow, a word or short phrase has been removed.

- Part 3 contains five short recordings of individuals speaking about a common subject. Each recording is followed by a multiple-choice question.

- Part 4 is a longer recording of an individual speaking about a specific topic. There follows seven multiple-choice questions.

In the exam, candidates will hear each recording twice and will be given time to read the questions before the recording is played. In this resource, the recordings play only once.

For more information, visit the Cambridge Assessment English website.

Prosperity Education

Our growing range of tests cover the IELTS Academic and Cambridge English B2 First (previously known as the FCE), C1 Advanced (CAE) and C2 Proficiency (CPE) exam. They are available in print or as pdfs which you can download directly from www.prosperityeducation.net. Each resource has a free sample so that you can evaluate its quality.

Cambridge B2 First Listening

Test 1

Cambridge B2 First Listening

Part 1   Test 1
                                                        Audio track: B2_Listening_1_1.mp3

You will hear people speaking in eight different situations. For questions 1–8, select the best answer A, B or C. Read the questions carefully before playing the audio. In the exam, you will have the opportunity to listen to each recording twice.

1   You hear two people talking about a department store called Murray's. What is the man complaining about?

   A   Product choice
   B   Customer service
   C   Opening hours

2   You hear a woman talking about photography on a radio show. What does she think about photo-editing software?

   A   People rely on it too much.
   B   It makes people less creative.
   C   It is difficult to use effectively.

3   You hear an announcement at the train station. What is the speaker doing?

   A   Promoting a service
   B   Making an apology
   C   Giving an update

4   You overhear two friends who have just been to a concert. What do they agree on?

   A   The concert was disappointing.
   B   The venue was unsuitable.
   C   The ticket price was too high.

Cambridge B2 First Listening

5 You hear two athletes talking about their new coach. How does the woman feel?

    A She is worried about the coach's expectations.
    B She is confused about the coach's methods.
    C She is enthusiastic about the coach's experience.

6 You hear a woman leaving a voicemail message. What is the problem?

    A She arrived late for her meeting.
    B The airline lost her luggage.
    C Her flight was cancelled.

7 You hear an interview with a film director on a podcast. What is unusual about his latest film?

    A The soundtrack
    B The cast
    C The subject

8 You overhear two friends talking in a restaurant. What is the woman doing?

    A Offering to share some dishes with the boy
    B Recommending a dish to the boy
    C Persuading the boy to order more dishes

Cambridge B2 First Listening

Part 2
Test 1
Audio track: B2_Listening_1_2.mp3

You will hear Aisha Hawkins, an architecture graduate, talking about her studies and career. For questions 9–18, complete the sentence with a word or short phrase (a maximum of three words). Read the questions carefully before playing the audio. In the exam, you will have the opportunity to listen to each recording twice.

Aisha always enjoyed school lessons which involved **9)**_____.

Aisha was inspired to train as an architect during a **10)**_____.

Her school tutors advised her to take additional **11)**_____ classes to help her prepare for university.

Aisha's parents were pleased when she decided to select the most **12)**_____ course.

Architecture students must be prepared for **13)**_____ that students on other programmes do not have.

Aisha says her degree was less challenging than the **14)**_____ afterwards.

Aisha chose her current position because it offered the best **15)**_____.

Her most enjoyable project so far has been designing a **16)**_____.

She most enjoys projects where she has a lot of **17)**_____.

Aisha says that **18)**_____ is the most important aspect of all design projects.

Cambridge B2 First Listening

Part 3

Test 1
Audio track: B2_Listening_1_3.mp3

You will hear five different people talking about eating out. For questions 19–23, select from the list (A–H) what each person speaks about. There are three extra statements which you do not have to use. Read the questions carefully before playing the audio. In the exam, you will have the opportunity to listen to each recording twice.

Which person speaks about:

A   preferring to make food at home

Speaker 1	19

B   struggling to feel comfortable in restaurants

Speaker 2	20

C   valuing good service

Speaker 3	21

D   trying unusual dishes

Speaker 4	22

E   deciding where to eat

Speaker 5	23

F   missing old-fashioned restaurants

G   paying the bill

H   ordering more than they need

Cambridge B2 First Listening

Part 4
Test 1
Audio track: B2_Listening_1_4.mp3

You will hear an interview with a psychologist called Helen Simpson, who is talking about mindfulness. For questions 24–30, select the best answer A, B or C. Read the questions carefully before playing the audio. In the exam, you will have the opportunity to listen to each recording twice.

24   What is the purpose of Dr Simpson's book?

    A Correcting some misunderstandings about mindfulness

    B Showing the practical uses of mindfulness

    C Explaining the reasons for the popularity of mindfulness.

25   Dr Simpson believes most people suffer from stress because they:

    A use technology too much.

    B find it difficult to manage their time.

    C try to do too many things at once.

26   What did the American study discover about 'mind-wandering'?

    A It makes people less happy.

    B It affects people's physical health.

    C It stops people being productive.

27   When did Dr Simpson become interested in mindfulness?

    A When she attended a seminar at a conference

    B While she was researching business professionals

    C While she was working in a high-pressure environment

28 What does Dr Simpson say about mindfulness training?

  A It involves focusing on an object.
  B It takes a lot of time to learn.
  C It requires all five senses.

29 When doing mindfulness exercises, most of her clients initially feel:

  A anxious.
  B embarrassed.
  C suspicious.

30 Dr Simpson suggests that all listeners should try:

  A focusing on their food more.
  B doing some new creative activities.
  C increasing their physical exercise.

Answer sheet: Cambridge B2 First Listening   Test No. [ ]

Mark out of 30 [ ]

Name _____   Date _____

Part 1:   8 marks

Mark the appropriate answer (A, B or C).   0 A **B** C

1 A B C   5 A B C
2 A B C   6 A B C
3 A B C   7 A B C
4 A B C   8 A B C

Part 2:   10 marks

Write your answers in capital letters, using one box per letter.

0 | B | E | C | A | U | S | E |

9
10
11
12
13
14
15
16
17
18

Answer sheet: Cambridge B2 First Listening

Part 3: 5 marks

Match the correct statement from the list (A-H).

| 0 | Speaker 1 | E |

19	Speaker 1	
20	Speaker 2	
21	Speaker 3	
22	Speaker 4	
23	Speaker 5	

Part 4: 7 marks

Mark the appropriate answer (A, B or C).

| 0 | A **B** C |

24	A B C
25	A B C
26	A B C
27	A B C
28	A B C
29	A B C
30	A B C

Cambridge B2 First Listening

Test 2

Cambridge B2 First Listening

Part 1
Test 2
Audio track: B2_Listening_2_1.mp3

You will hear people speaking in eight different situations. For questions 1–8, select the best answer A, B or C. Read the questions carefully before playing the audio. In the exam, you will have the opportunity to listen to each recording twice.

1   You hear two students talking about student life. What is the girl disappointed with?

     A   The quality of the teaching

     B   The content of her course

     C   The facilities at the college

2   You hear a woman talking about being a chef. What does she think has been the most important development in her industry?

     A   Changes in the way professional chefs train

     B   The development of alternatives to meat

     C   The growing influence of celebrity TV chefs

3   You hear an announcement at a supermarket. What is on sale for a special price at the moment?

     A   Butter

     B   Bread

     C   Cheese

4   You hear part of a radio interview. What is the interviewer doing?

     A   Encouraging the politician to provide a personal opinion

     B   Explaining why the politician's statistics are incorrect

     C   Asking the politician to provide a clearer answer

5 You overhear two fans talking about their football club. How does the boy feel?

    A He is excited about the club's new players.

    B He is confident that the club will be successful soon.

    C He is impressed by the coach's training methods.

6 Your cousin has left a voicemail message about a trip. What does your cousin want to do?

    A Change the dates of the trip

    B Book the main activities in advance

    C Find cheaper accommodation

7 You overhear two people discussing a problem. What do they decide to do?

    A Complain to the police

    B Talk to their neighbour

    C Contact the authorities

8 You hear an expert talking on the radio about antiques. What advice does he give the listeners?

    A Choose where to sell your objects carefully

    B Buy unusual objects made by local producers

    C Invest more in good quality objects

Cambridge B2 First Listening

Part 2 Test 2
Audio track: B2_Listening_2_2.mp3

You will hear Carl Johnson, a company director, talking about his business. For questions 9–18, complete the sentence with a word or short phrase (a maximum of three words). Read the questions carefully before playing the audio. In the exam, you will have the opportunity to listen to each recording twice.

Carl's company specialises in doing **9)**_____ from the air.

In the past, the technology Carl uses was originally intended just for **10)**_____ purposes.

Scientists use the same technology to find evidence of **11)**_____ when they're studying wide areas of land.

Carl thinks people are beginning to see the **12)**_____ of the technology he uses.

Carl mainly works with clients involved in **13)**_____.

He is now helping some American companies check the quality of their **14)**_____.

He thinks the growing interest in his industry is due to the **15)**_____ of the devices.

His latest product is his **16)**_____ to help people interested in using the devices.

Carl thinks social media users are keen to use the devices to help them post things that **17)**_____ compared to other people's content.

Carl is in favour of having more laws to protect people's **18)**_____.

Cambridge B2 First Listening

Part 3

Test 2
Audio track: B2_Listening_2_3.mp3

You will hear five different people talking about advertising. For questions 19–23, select from the list (A–H) what each person speaks about. There are three extra statements which you do not have to use. Read the questions carefully before playing the audio. In the exam, you will have the opportunity to listen to each recording twice.

Which person speaks about:

A supporting stricter controls on advertising

| | Speaker 1 | | **19** |

B finding pop-up advertising effective

| | Speaker 2 | | **20** |

C preferring advertising that is funny

| | Speaker 3 | | **21** |

D wanting to work in advertising

| | Speaker 4 | | **22** |

E advertising being part of culture

| | Speaker 5 | | **23** |

F wanting less advertising in public places

G not trusting advertising

H being concerned about the effects of advertising

Cambridge B2 First Listening

Part 4
Test 2
Audio track: B2_Listening_2_4.mp3

You will hear an interview with a woman called Louise Harper, who works as a hotel manager in Malta. For questions 24–30, select the best answer A, B or C. Read the questions carefully before playing the audio. In the exam, you will have the opportunity to listen to each recording twice.

24 What does Louise see as the most important part of her job?

   A   Keeping her customers happy
   B   Developing her staff's skills
   C   Identifying new opportunities

25 What originally attracted Louise to working in Malta?

   A   She wanted a better quality of life.
   B   She had family in the country.
   C   She was offered a great job.

26 On working in Malta, Louise says:

   A   she is optimistic about her long-term prospects.
   B   there are more opportunities than she had expected.
   C   her sector is still relatively undeveloped.

27 What type of tourism does Louise think will become more popular?

   A   Short city breaks
   B   Adventure holidays
   C   Luxury travel

28 How does Louise feel about the development of eco-tourism?

   A Hopeful about its potential impact
   B Disappointed about its lack of popularity
   C Confused about its main aims

29 What advice does Louise give to tourists planning their holiday?

   A Don't travel in peak times
   B Don't over-plan the trip
   C Don't use online reviews

30 In the long-term, Louise hopes to:

   A open a chain of hotels.
   B return to her home country.
   C work as a tourism consultant.

Answer sheet: Cambridge B2 First Listening

Test No.

Mark out of 30

Name _____ **Date** _____

Part 1: 8 marks

Mark the appropriate answer (A, B or C). | 0 | A **B** C |

1	A B C		5	A B C
2	A B C		6	A B C
3	A B C		7	A B C
4	A B C		8	A B C

Part 2: 10 marks

Write your answers in capital letters, using one box per letter.

| 0 | B | E | C | A | U | S | E | | | |

9.
10.
11.
12.
13.
14.
15.
16.
17.
18.

Answer sheet: Cambridge B2 First Listening

Part 3: 5 marks

Match the correct statement from the list (A-H).

0	Speaker 1	E

19	Speaker 1	
20	Speaker 2	
21	Speaker 3	
22	Speaker 4	
23	Speaker 5	

Part 4: 7 marks

Mark the appropriate answer (A, B or C).

0	A **B** C

24	A B C
25	A B C
26	A B C
27	A B C
28	A B C
29	A B C
30	A B C

Cambridge B2 First Listening

Test 3

Cambridge B2 First Listening

Part 1   Test 3
                                                       Audio track: B2_Listening_3_1.mp3

You will hear people speaking in eight different situations. For questions 1–8, select the best answer A, B or C. Read the questions carefully before playing the audio. In the exam, you will have the opportunity to listen to each recording twice.

1   You hear two colleagues talking about a work project. Which aspect of the project do they disagree about?

   A   The design they should use
   B   The budget they should have
   C   The team they should hire

2   You overhear a woman leaving a voicemail about a shopping trip. How did she feel during the trip?

   A   Disappointed with the quality of products
   B   Embarrassed about asking for discounts
   C   Shocked at the prices of wedding items

3   You overhear a conversation between two gym employees. What are the speakers complaining about?

   A   Lack of equipment
   B   Poor changing rooms
   C   Cancellation of classes

4   You overhear a conversation between two neighbours. What does the woman want her neighbour to do for her event?

   A   Make some items
   B   Advertise her event
   C   Donate some money

5 You overhear a woman leaving a voicemail about a business meeting. What does the woman say about the meeting?

    A The meeting achieved very little.

    B The company made her feel unwelcome.

    C The manager was unprepared.

6 You hear a radio presenter talking about a film. What is the presenter doing?

    A Asking for listeners' views on the film

    B Explaining the plot of the film

    C Describing how he felt about the film

7 You overhear two friends discussing a book. What do they agree about?

    A The author's reputation is growing.

    B The author's previous novel was better.

    C The author's strength is in his characters.

8 You hear a man speaking on a telephone. What is he trying to do?

    A Change his purchase

    B Make a payment

    C Ask for a refund

Cambridge B2 First Listening

Part 2   Test 3
                                                        Audio track: B2_Listening_3_2.mp3

You will hear a radio presenter giving information about a film festival. For questions 9–18, complete the sentence with a word or short phrase (a maximum of three words). Read the questions carefully before playing the audio. In the exam, you will have the opportunity to listen to each recording twice.

The festival was founded by a film **9)**_____.

The original purpose of the festival was to promote **10)**_____ cinema.

There are strict rules about the **11)**_____ of films entered into the competitions.

The presenter is pleased about the new award category for **12)**_____ films.

The **13)**_____ award is determined by the general public.

All films shown at the festival are selected for their **14)**_____.

The presenter approves of the festival's **15)**_____ and its commitment to doing good.

Local **16)**_____ receive a portion of the festival's profits.

Compared to similar events, the presenter enjoys the **17)**_____ of this festival.

Visitors have many opportunities to meet the **18)**_____ during the festival, which is unusual.

Cambridge B2 First Listening

Part 3

Test 3
Audio track: B2_Listening_3_3.mp3

You will hear five different people talking about school trips. For questions 19–23, select from the list (A–H) what each person speaks about. There are three extra statements which you do not have to use. Read the questions carefully before playing the audio. In the exam, you will have the opportunity to listen to each recording twice.

Which person speaks about:

A   preferring cultural school trips

Speaker 1	19

B   being enthusiastic about school trips

Speaker 2	20

C   finding school trips disappointing

Speaker 3	21

D   feeling homesick on a school trip

Speaker 4	22

E   wanting schools to change their school trips

Speaker 5	23

F   doubting the educational value of school trips

G   not enjoying the food on a school trip

H   getting into trouble on a school trip

Cambridge B2 First Listening

Part 4   Test 3
                                                              Audio track: B2_Listening_3_4.mp3

You will hear an interview with a man called Rob Jackson, who works in the car industry. For questions 24–30, select the best answer A, B or C. Read the questions carefully before playing the audio. In the exam, you will have the opportunity to listen to each recording twice.

24   Sales in Rob's company are growing fastest in:

   A   Asia.
   B   North America.
   C   Europe.

25   How does Rob feel about hybrid-electric cars?

   A   Concerned that they might confuse consumers
   B   Convinced that they will become more popular
   C   Doubtful that they can help the environment

26   What is Rob responsible for in his job?

   A   Vehicle marketing
   B   Vehicle battery
   C   Vehicle appearance

27   What is the main source of business for Rob's company?

   A   Older motorists
   B   People with children
   C   Urban professionals

28 Rob thinks electric vehicle sales are mainly influenced by:

   A the price of electric vehicles.

   B the availability of charging stations.

   C interest in environmental issues.

29 Rob is currently doing some research on:

   A people's use of car-sharing apps.

   B consumers' attitudes to electric cars.

   C cars' energy consumption in different temperatures.

30 Rob enjoys his current role because:

   A there is always something new to learn.

   B he has opportunities to work overseas.

   C the company offers great financial benefits.

Answer sheet: Cambridge B2 First Listening

Test No.

Mark out of 30

Name _____ Date _____

Part 1:

8 marks

Mark the appropriate answer (A, B or C).   0 A **B** C

1 A B C   5 A B C
2 A B C   6 A B C
3 A B C   7 A B C
4 A B C   8 A B C

Part 2:

10 marks

Write your answers in capital letters, using one box per letter.

0 | B | E | C | A | U | S | E

9
10
11
12
13
14
15
16
17
18

Answer sheet: Cambridge B2 First Listening

Part 3: 5 marks

Match the correct statement from the list (A-H).

| 0 | Speaker 1 | E |

19	Speaker 1	
20	Speaker 2	
21	Speaker 3	
22	Speaker 4	
23	Speaker 5	

Part 4: 7 marks

Mark the appropriate answer (A, B or C).

| 0 | A **B** C |

24	A B C
25	A B C
26	A B C
27	A B C
28	A B C
29	A B C
30	A B C

Cambridge B2 First Listening

Test 4

Cambridge B2 First Listening

Part 1 Test 4
Audio track: B2_Listening_4_1.mp3

You will hear people speaking in eight different situations. For questions 1–8, select the best answer A, B or C. Read the questions carefully before playing the audio. In the exam, you will have the opportunity to listen to each recording twice.

1   You hear two people talking about a restaurant meal. Why is the woman annoyed?

    A   The food took a long time to arrive.

    B   The restaurant cancelled her booking.

    C   The man arrived late for the meal.

2   You hear a woman talking about leisure activities. Which activity does she feel she has benefitted from the most?

    A   Gardening

    B   Singing

    C   Climbing

3   You overhear a conversation in a shop. What does the customer tell the shop assistant?

    A   The customer has lost their receipt.

    B   The shop sent the wrong product.

    C   The product arrived too late.

4   You hear a woman presenting on a TV show. What is she talking about?

    A   How to use a particular ingredient

    B   Where to buy a particular ingredient

    C   What to use instead of a particular ingredient

5 You hear two businesspeople talking about a work project. How does the man feel?

    A Concerned that the project will go over budget

    B Surprised that the project will go ahead

    C Relieved that he will be involved in the project

6 You hear a sports commentary on the radio. What is the reporter doing?

    A Describing the atmosphere in the stadium

    B Criticising some of the fans' behaviour

    C Explaining the importance of the match

7 You overhear two friends talking about a hair salon. What does Marco's Salon regularly do?

    A Use inexperienced staff

    B Overcharge for its services

    C Try to sell unnecessary products

8 You hear a conversation between two friends talking about a college open day. What course has the girl chosen?

    A Medicine

    B Biology

    C Engineering

Cambridge B2 First Listening

Part 2
Test 4
Audio track: B2_Listening_4_2.mp3

You will hear Donna Jackson, a professor, giving a lecture about the Hippocratic Oath. For questions 9–18, complete the sentence with a word or short phrase (a maximum of three words). Read the questions carefully before playing the audio. In the exam, you will have the opportunity to listen to each recording twice.

A key part of Professor Jackson's work is **9)**_____.

She wants the audience to get involved in some **10)**_____ activities during the lecture.

She says it's essential for healthcare professionals to **11)**_____ their patients.

The Hippocratic Oath is a kind of **12)**_____ for medical professionals.

Swearing by the Oath is not **13)**_____ in most medical schools now.

One of the most well-known concepts associated with the Oath is that healthcare professionals must **14)**_____.

Professor Jackson feels very strongly that healthcare systems must emphasise **15)**_____.

She believes that effective healthcare starts with good **16)**_____.

People working in healthcare must be able to **17)**_____ all key decisions.

Professor Jackson says that all medical guidelines reflect the **18)**_____ of society at that time.

Cambridge B2 First Listening

Part 3
Test 4
Audio track: B2_Listening_4_3.mp3

You will hear five different people talking about their use of social media. For questions 19–23, select from the list (A–H) what each person speaks about. There are three extra statements which you do not have to use. Read the questions carefully before playing the audio. In the exam, you will have the opportunity to listen to each recording twice.

Which person speaks about:

A worrying about their appearance

B social media being difficult to trust

C being slow to get into social media

D using social media mainly to share selfies

E widening their social network

F social media making them more aware of social issues

G deciding to reduce their usage of social media

H worrying about young people looking at social media images

Speaker 1		19
Speaker 2		20
Speaker 3		21
Speaker 4		22
Speaker 5		23

Cambridge B2 First Listening

Part 4

Test 4
Audio track: B2_Listening_4_4.mp3

You will hear an interview with a consumer expert called Nigel Wilkins, who is talking about money. For questions 24–30, select the best answer A, B or C. Read the questions carefully before playing the audio. In the exam, you will have the opportunity to listen to each recording twice.

24 Nigel's new TV show is mainly for:

   A teachers.

   B parents.

   C teenagers.

25 Why does Nigel believe his show is popular?

   A It treats serious subjects in an entertaining way.

   B It mainly focuses on unusual subjects.

   C It covers subjects that viewers ask for.

26 What policy does Nigel support?

   A Changing the age limits for credit cards

   B Providing financial education classes at school

   C Banning advertising in video games

27 Nigel thinks consumer habits have mainly changed because:

   A people prefer saving their money nowadays.

   B there is growing interest in luxury lifestyles.

   C it is becoming easier to get credit cards.

28 How does Nigel feel about modern shopping habits?

  A Confused that people want to shop so often
  B Annoyed that the quality of products is decreasing
  C Concerned that society focuses on the wrong things

29 Nigel recently presented a programme about:

  A recycled products.
  B repair shops.
  C product exchanges.

30 Nigel has decided to:

  A work in politics.
  B write a children's book.
  C continue his TV show.

Answer sheet: Cambridge B2 First Listening   Test No. ☐

Mark out of 30 ☐

Name _____   Date _____

Part 1:   8 marks

Mark the appropriate answer (A, B or C).   0 A **B** C

1	A B C		5	A B C
2	A B C		6	A B C
3	A B C		7	A B C
4	A B C		8	A B C

Part 2:   10 marks

Write your answers in capital letters, using one box per letter.

0 | B E C A U S E

9
10
11
12
13
14
15
16
17
18

Answer sheet: Cambridge B2 First Listening

Part 3: 5 marks

Match the correct statement from the list (A-H).

| 0 | Speaker 1 | E |

19	Speaker 1	
20	Speaker 2	
21	Speaker 3	
22	Speaker 4	
23	Speaker 5	

Part 4: 7 marks

Mark the appropriate answer (A, B or C).

| 0 | A | **B** | C |

24	A	B	C
25	A	B	C
26	A	B	C
27	A	B	C
28	A	B	C
29	A	B	C
30	A	B	C

Cambridge B2 First Listening

Test 5

Cambridge B2 First Listening

Part 1   Test 5
                                                       Audio track: B2_Listening_5_1.mp3

You will hear people speaking in eight different situations. For questions 1–8, select the best answer A, B or C. Read the questions carefully before playing the audio. In the exam, you will have the opportunity to listen to each recording twice.

1   You hear two people talking about their favourite football team. What does the girl say is the team's main strength?

    A   The amount of effort given by the team
    B   The playing style of the team
    C   The level of experience within the team

2   You hear a woman talking about travelling with friends. What does she think is the most useful piece of advice?

    A   Learn to compromise
    B   Share the costs
    C   Spend time apart

3   You hear an announcement at a concert venue. What problem is being explained?

    A   The concert has to finish early.
    B   The concert has been cancelled.
    C   The concert will be delayed.

4   You hear a woman talking on a TV show. What is she talking about?

    A   A film
    B   A book
    C   A play

Cambridge B2 First Listening

5 You hear two band members talking about their new singer. How does the woman feel?

   A She is impressed with the singer's own songs.
   B She is keen to record some songs with the singer.
   C She is worried about the singer's lack of ambition.

6 You hear two people at a social event. What is the woman doing?

   A Politely declining a business offer
   B Describing her business background
   C Making a business recommendation

7 You overhear a husband and wife who have just come back from a holiday. What do they agree on?

   A The food was too expensive.
   B The holiday was very relaxing.
   C The accommodation was disappointing.

8 You hear a trainer talking to a client at the gym. What is he trying to do?

   A Demonstrate a new exercise
   B Motivate his client to exercise more
   C Correct his client's mistakes

Cambridge B2 First Listening

Part 2

Test 5
Audio track: B2_Listening_5_2.mp3

You will hear Julia Richards, a local official, giving a presentation about the proposed development of a new business park. For questions 9–18, complete the sentence with a word or short phrase (a maximum of three words). Read the questions carefully before playing the audio. In the exam, you will have the opportunity to listen to each recording twice.

Julia believes that the business park has the potential to lead to better 9)_____ in the local area.

The business park will be particularly important for the 10)_____.

She predicts that the 11)_____ of the business park will be seen within five years.

She is 12)_____ that the project managers are protecting local wildlife.

Julia says significant amounts of 13)_____ will be generated by the business park, which will benefit the local area.

Julia wants to talk about the negative 14)_____ surrounding the project.

Building most of the new construction on the 15)_____ of the site will reduce disruption.

Julia is campaigning for better 16)_____ options.

She wants volunteers to help her 17)_____ as part of her campaign.

Julia says that local residents are in an ideal position to 18)_____ the project.

Cambridge B2 First Listening

Part 3

Test 5
Audio track: B2_Listening_5_3.mp3

You will hear five different people talking about their hobbies. For questions 19–23, select from the list (A–H) what each person speaks about. There are three extra statements which you do not have to use. Read the questions carefully before playing the audio. In the exam, you will have the opportunity to listen to each recording twice.

Which person speaks about:

- **A** getting bored of their hobbies easily
- **B** gaining confidence from their hobbies
- **C** meeting new people through their hobbies
- **D** having an unusual hobby
- **E** their hobby becoming too expensive
- **F** struggling to find time for hobbies
- **G** going back to a previous hobby
- **H** preferring to focus on one main hobby

Speaker 1 [ ] 19

Speaker 2 [ ] 20

Speaker 3 [ ] 21

Speaker 4 [ ] 22

Speaker 5 [ ] 23

Cambridge B2 First Listening

Part 4   Test 5
                                                              Audio track: B2_Listening_5_4.mp3

You will hear an interview with a scientist called Mark Richards, who studies weather patterns. For questions 24–30, select the best answer A, B or C. Read the questions carefully before playing the audio. In the exam, you will have the opportunity to listen to each recording twice.

24 When Mark talks about his work, most people:
    A are surprised to discover its importance.
    B want to know how to get involved.
    C find it difficult to understand what he does.

25 Mark chose his particular field because:
    A he had enjoyed studying it at university.
    B it was the newest area of climate science.
    C there were so many questions to investigate.

26 What subject is Mark researching at the moment?
    A What determines the size of a cloud
    B Why clouds differ around the world
    C How temperature affects clouds

27 What does Mark say about 'citizen science' projects?
    A They can help scientists conduct their research quickly.
    B They can produce large amounts of useful data.
    C They can prove whether scientists' theories are correct.

28 Why is satellite technology unsuitable for Mark's current research?

    A This type of equipment costs too much to use.

    B The project is based in an area with a lot of snow.

    C The research requires information taken from the ground.

29 Mark says most of the volunteers he works with:

    A are interested in the subject of climate change.

    B already have a background in science.

    C work on the project for several months.

30 What does Mark like most about his broadcasting career?

    A Sharing knowledge with a wide audience

    B Changing people's views of science

    C Getting the chance to learn about new topics

Answer sheet: Cambridge B2 First Listening   Test No. ☐

Mark out of 30 ☐

Name _____   **Date** _____

Part 1:   8 marks

Mark the appropriate answer (A, B or C).   0 A **B** C

1	A B C		5	A B C
2	A B C		6	A B C
3	A B C		7	A B C
4	A B C		8	A B C

Part 2:   10 marks

Write your answers in capital letters, using one box per letter.

0 | B | E | C | A | U | S | E | | | |

9
10
11
12
13
14
15
16
17
18

Answer sheet: Cambridge B2 First Listening

Part 3: 5 marks

Match the correct statement from the list (A-H).

0	Speaker 1	E

19	Speaker 1	
20	Speaker 2	
21	Speaker 3	
22	Speaker 4	
23	Speaker 5	

Part 4: 7 marks

Mark the appropriate answer (A, B or C).

0	A	**B**	C

24	A	B	C
25	A	B	C
26	A	B	C
27	A	B	C
28	A	B	C
29	A	B	C
30	A	B	C

Cambridge B2 First Listening

Test 6

Cambridge B2 First Listening

Part 1　　　　　　　　　　　　　　　　　　　　　　　　　　　　　　Test 6
　　　　　　　　　　　　　　　　　　　　　Audio track: B2_Listening_6_1.mp3

You will hear people speaking in eight different situations. For questions 1–8, select the best answer A, B or C. Read the questions carefully before playing the audio. In the exam, you will have the opportunity to listen to each recording twice.

1　You hear two people talking about a job interview. Why is the man disappointed?

　　A　He didn't perform well in the interview.
　　B　The position wasn't what he'd expected.
　　C　They didn't like his presentation.

2　You hear a woman on the radio talking about houseplants. What does she think is the main mistake people make with houseplants?

　　A　Letting them grow too large
　　B　Putting them in the wrong place
　　C　Watering them too often

3　You overhear a conversation in a clothes shop. What is the problem?

　　A　The store does not accept credit cards.
　　B　The assistant has made a mistake with the bill.
　　C　The customer has ordered the wrong item.

4　You hear two students talking about a lesson they have just had. What did they learn in today's lesson?

　　A　Which tasks are required for their projects
　　B　What subjects to focus on in their projects
　　C　How to find information for their projects

5 You hear a man talking to his friend about a gift he has received. How does he feel about the gift?

   A Keen to get rid of the gift

   B Worried about what the gift might mean

   C Embarrassed about receiving the gift

6 You hear a woman leaving a voicemail for her classmate. What is the woman doing?

   A Comparing some options

   B Asking for some advice

   C Reporting some opinions

7 You overhear two friends talking about a wedding. What do they agree on?

   A There were too many guests.

   B The location was amazing.

   C The entertainment was weird.

8 You hear a man leaving a voicemail message. What is he talking about?

   A Where he will meet someone

   B Why he will be late

   C What transport he will use

Cambridge B2 First Listening

Part 2

Test 6
Audio track: B2_Listening_6_2.mp3

You will hear Dr Olivia Freeman, an education expert, talking about children's playgrounds. For questions 9–18, complete the sentence with a word or short phrase (a maximum of three words). Read the questions carefully before playing the audio. In the exam, you will have the opportunity to listen to each recording twice.

Dr Freeman's original research focused on how playing areas can affect children's **9)**_____.

She discovered that children who spent more time playing in these areas were less **10)**_____ .

The main benefit she noticed was the higher levels of **11)**_____ in children who had regular access to playgrounds.

Teachers have reported that playgrounds encourage children to be more **12)**_____, which can improve their learning.

Her second study compared the **13)**_____ offered by different types of playground equipment.

She recommends equipment called **14)**_____ to help children develop upper-body strength.

Dr Freeman says playgrounds are particularly important for children living in **15)**_____.

She now works as a consultant to help **16)**_____ design playground areas.

She believes that **17)**_____ is the key to a good playground design.

She supports the use of **18)**_____ materials in play areas.

Cambridge B2 First Listening

Part 3

Test 6
Audio track: B2_Listening_6_3.mp3

You will hear five different people talking about the devices they own. For questions 19–23, select from the list (A–H) what each person speaks about. There are three extra statements which you do not have to use. Read the questions carefully before playing the audio. In the exam, you will have the opportunity to listen to each recording twice.

Which person speaks about:

A missing a device they used to own

B being the first to try new technology

C finding devices practical and nice to look at

D wanting to upgrade one of their devices

E winning their favourite device

F saving up for a device

G becoming too dependent on technology

H using technology to improve their health

Speaker 1 — 19

Speaker 2 — 20

Speaker 3 — 21

Speaker 4 — 22

Speaker 5 — 23

Cambridge B2 First Listening

Part 4

Test 6

Audio track: B2_Listening_6_4.mp3

You will hear an interview with a university professor called Rachel Sanders, who is talking about history. For questions 24–30, select the best answer A, B or C. Read the questions carefully before playing the audio. In the exam, you will have the opportunity to listen to each recording twice.

24 Rachel says the main purpose of the university festival is:

   A to encourage people to become interested in local history.

   B to promote the history courses offered at the university.

   C to celebrate the life of an important historical figure.

25 What has Rachel's team been trying to discover in Barton Kirk?

   A Why the site had religious importance

   B When the site was founded

   C Whether people lived there

26 Rachel says the hardest aspect of the research project has been:

   A dealing with unexpected weather conditions.

   B using ancient objects to understand the past.

   C protecting the site from damage.

27 What will visitors have a chance to do at Rachel's festival event?

   A Play some instruments

   B Listen to some poetry

   C Try some recipes

28 What has been the proudest moment in Rachel's career?

   A Becoming head of her department
   B Winning a teaching award
   C Writing her first book

29 What is the focus of Rachel's new course at the university?

   A Using computers in historical research
   B Preserving historical buildings
   C Analysing historical documents

30 How does Rachel feel about tourism at historical sites?

   A She is convinced it is unlikely to grow.
   B She thinks it is hard to organise effectively.
   C She doubts it has educational benefits.

Answer sheet: Cambridge B2 First Listening   Test No. ☐

Mark out of 30 ☐

Name _____   **Date** _____

Part 1:   8 marks

Mark the appropriate answer (A, B or C).   0 A **B** C

1 A B C   5 A B C
2 A B C   6 A B C
3 A B C   7 A B C
4 A B C   8 A B C

Part 2:   10 marks

Write your answers in capital letters, using one box per letter.

0 B E C A U S E

9
10
11
12
13
14
15
16
17
18

Answer sheet: Cambridge B2 First Listening

Part 3:   5 marks

Match the correct statement from the list (A-H).

| 0 | Speaker 1 | E |

19	Speaker 1	
20	Speaker 2	
21	Speaker 3	
22	Speaker 4	
23	Speaker 5	

Part 4:   7 marks

Mark the appropriate answer (A, B or C).

| 0 | A | **B** | C |

24	A	B	C
25	A	B	C
26	A	B	C
27	A	B	C
28	A	B	C
29	A	B	C
30	A	B	C

Cambridge B2 First Listening

Answers

Cambridge B2 First Listening   Answers

Test 1   Test 1

Part 1

1	B	2	A	3	C	4	B
5	A	6	B	7	C	8	C

Part 2

9	solving problems / problem-solving
10	school trip
11	maths
12	flexible
13	expenses
14	qualifying exams
15	training / training opportunities
16	library / city library
17	input
18	compromise

Part 3

19	D	20	H	21	E
22	C	23	B		

Part 4

24	B	25	C	26	A
27	C	28	A	29	B
30	A				

Answers

Test 2

Part 1							
1	C	2	B	3	B	4	A
5	A	6	C	7	C	8	A

Part 2	
9	photography / aerial photography
10	military
11	environmental changes
12	potential / commercial potential
13	film production
14	crops
15	falling price / price
16	course / online course
17	stand out
18	privacy

Part 3					
19	B	20	G	21	D
22	A	23	E		

Part 4							
24	C	25	B	26	A		
27	B	28	A	29	B		
30	C						

Cambridge B2 First Listening

Test 3

Part 1

1	B	2	B	3	C	4	A
5	C	6	A	7	B	8	A

Part 2

9	critic
10	independent
11	budgets
12	animation
13	Golden Heart
14	social impact
15	sponsorship policy
16	film schools
17	atmosphere
18	performers

Part 3

19	D	20	H	21	B
22	F	23	A		

Part 4

24	C	25	A	26	B
27	C	28	B	29	A
30	A				

Answers

Test 4

Part 1							
1	B	2	C	3	A	4	A
5	B	6	A	7	C	8	B

Part 2	
9	training doctors / training new doctors
10	drama
11	respect
12	moral code
13	compulsory
14	do no harm
15	teamwork
16	communication
17	justify
18	values

Part 3					
19	C	20	E	21	F
22	G	23	H		

Part 4					
24	C	25	A	26	B
27	B	28	C	29	B
30	B				

Cambridge B2 First Listening

Test 5

Part 1

1	B	2	C	3	B	4	A
5	B	6	A	7	C	8	C

Part 2

9	employment opportunities / opportunities
10	IT sector
11	economic benefits / benefits
12	relieved
13	solar power
14	publicity
15	west side
16	public transport
17	collect data
18	improve

Part 3

19	B	20	F	21	A
22	D	23	G		

Part 4

24	A	25	C	26	A
27	B	28	C	29	A
30	B				

Answers

Test 6

Part 1							
1	B	2	C	3	A	4	C
5	B	6	C	7	B	8	A

Part 2	
9	social skills
10	selfish
11	confidence
12	creative
13	physical benefits
14	monkey bars
15	urban areas
16	councils
17	variety
18	recycled

Part 3					
19	B	20	H	21	E
22	A	23	D		

Part 4					
24	A	25	C	26	B
27	C	28	B	29	A
30	C				

Cambridge B2 First Listening

Transcripts

Cambridge B2 First Listening

Test 1

Part 1
Audio track: B2_Listening_1_1.mp3

Part 1. You will hear people talking in eight different situations. For questions 1 to 8, you must choose the best answer: A, B or C.

Question 1 **You hear two people talking about a department store called Murray's. What is the man complaining about?**

Speaker 1 Have you shopped at Murrays recently? I can't believe how much it's changed.

Speaker 2 Not for years! Have they still got their amazing toy department? Going there when I was a kid used to be such a treat!

Speaker 1 Well, I doubt you'd enjoy it now. They've still got some decent products, but all the staff look so miserable.

Speaker 2 Well, they're standing on their feet all day, having to deal with demanding customers. Don't forget they're open much later than other places in town. They're probably exhausted!

Speaker 1 That's no excuse! If they're going to be rude, I'll just stick to shopping online.

Question 2 **You hear a woman talking about photography on a radio show. What does she think about photo-editing software?**

Now, a growing number of people wouldn't dream of sharing their pictures online until they've been enhanced using photo-editing software. And the different effects you can achieve with this technology are really stunning. It's great to see people experimenting with what the software can do, but let's be honest: most of us can tell when images have been edited, can't we? And I do worry that people just end up depending heavily on digital editing rather than trying to take good photos in the first place.

Question 3 **You hear an announcement at the train station. What is the speaker doing?**

Due to adverse weather conditions in the eastern region, we regret to inform passengers that several services are running late, including all coastal line services. Passengers are advised to check the screens in the main hall for further information, or download the station app to get the most up-to-date travel information. As a result of these delays, the 10:15 service to Whitebeach will now depart from Platform 2. And we also politely remind passengers not to leave their luggage unattended on the platforms. Thank you.

Question 4 **You overhear two friends who have just been to a concert. What do they agree on?**

Speaker 1 Well, that wasn't what I'd expected at all!

Speaker 2 It sounds like you weren't impressed. I thought they were brilliant!

Transcripts

Speaker 1	Don't get me wrong, I enjoyed it. But they didn't have the same energy they have in their videos.
Speaker 2	Well, there's not much you can do in such a small space, is there? I mean, the way they perform definitely suits much larger theatres.
Speaker 1	Yes, I'm surprised they agreed to play at the local café. I don't think it worked.
Speaker 2	You're right, but this was just a charity gig, so we can't really expect much. For the amount they were charging, I think they were amazing.

Question 5   **You hear two athletes talking about their new coach. How does the woman feel?**

Speaker 1	I see you're working with Mel Phillips. She really knows her stuff, doesn't she? You'll learn so much from her.
Speaker 2	Everyone keeps saying that! I know she's coached so many champions, but it's still early days so let's wait and see.
Speaker 1	Well, you'll need to put the work in.
Speaker 2	Tell me about it! Our first training session was far harder than anything I've ever done before. I don't think she was very impressed with me. What if I never reach the level she wants?
Speaker 1	Mel's like that with everyone. She's got really high standards, so she's hard to please. But you'll be fine.
Speaker 2	Oh, I hope you're right.

Question 6   **You hear a woman leaving a voicemail message. What is the problem?**

Hi Rob, it's Alison. It's been a total disaster today. I arrived in London okay, but my bags didn't! I've called the airline and they're to trying to find out what's happened. They can't find any record of my bags being loaded onto my connecting flight, so they're not sure if they're in Dubai or if they're still in Bangkok. I'm so angry! Could you call the client and explain what's happened? I mean, I have my laptop, fortunately, but I can't go to the meeting in my travel clothes, can I? And worse, I won't be able to show them our products.

Question 7   **You hear an interview with a film director on a podcast. What is unusual about his latest film?**

Speaker 1	Today's guest is Max Frost, who's here to talk about his latest film 'The Last Road'. It's a great film, Max, and fans will be delighted to see some familiar faces…
Speaker 2	Thanks, yes, I was so lucky to work with Robert Jones and Anya Merton again. They're fantastic performers.
Speaker 1	But 'The Last Road' isn't a typical Max Frost film, is it?
Speaker 2	Well, it's still got many of the things I'm known for, like my use of special effects and music. But, yes, 'The Last Road' is certainly more serious in tone. And it's about farming, which isn't something that you usually see on cinema screens!

Cambridge B2 First Listening

Question 8 **You overhear two friends talking in a restaurant. What is the woman doing?**

Speaker 1 Have you chosen yet? I'm definitely getting the pasta and a few side dishes too. They do an amazing potato salad.

Speaker 2 I'm not sure. I quite fancy a salad, but I'm pretty hungry.

Speaker 1 Honestly, that won't be enough. You know that the portions here are quite small. Anyway, you always complain that you haven't ordered enough, and then you try to steal some of mine!

Speaker 2 Well, maybe we should just get a selection of dishes to enjoy together?

Speaker 1 No, I'd rather not because we have different tastes. But you should definitely get a burger or something to go with the salad.

Part 2

Audio track: B2_Listening_1_2.mp3

Part 2. You hear Aisha Hawkins, an architecture graduate, talking about her studies and career. For questions 9 to 18, complete the sentences with a word or short phrase.

Being an architect is definitely the right career for me, but strangely it wasn't something I'd always dreamt of doing. I mean, at school I used to enjoy solving problems in class. I knew I wanted a job which involved doing that, but I thought I'd end up doing something like medicine.

Actually, I didn't really know anything about architecture until I went to Barcelona when I was about 13 or 14. It was a school trip, not a family holiday, and we were there to study the architecture. Seeing all the amazing, unusual buildings really inspired me. So, really, that was when I decided I wanted to become an architect.

My teachers gave me some excellent advice about applying to university architecture programmes. They suggested I should do extra maths classes before starting my degree. I'm glad I listened to them because doing that really helped me prepare for my university classes.

And of course, I discussed my university plans with my parents too! They helped me compare the benefits of full-time courses and online degrees, but obviously I had to make the final decision. I decided to find a course that was as flexible as possible, and my parents were very happy about that. They'd been a little concerned that an architecture degree might be too limiting if I decided to do something else later.

One thing I'd say to any student thinking about doing an architecture degree is that you need to consider the financial side very carefully. You'll have expenses that other students won't have to deal with. So it's important to be prepared for that.

Something many people don't realise is that you don't automatically become an architect just by completing a degree. I loved doing my degree and learnt a lot from it, but I knew that if I wanted to work as an architect, I'd also need to pass qualifying exams afterwards. Those are even harder than the degree, and you take them after completing some practical training.

I'm now fully qualified and working for a firm of architects in London. Before I chose this role, I was actually offered positions with several different companies. Some of them offered a better salary than my current role, but I think I made the right choice. None of those companies offered any good training opportunities, and I think that's essential for newly qualified architects. I love my role because I always have the chance to develop my skills.

There's so much variety in my job. I can't imagine ever getting bored! One day I'm

Transcripts

designing government buildings, the next, a family home. If I had to choose my favourite project so far, it would probably be one I did last year. I was part of the team that designed a city library.

It might not sound very interesting, but there was actually a lot to think about. And what made it particularly enjoyable is that I had a lot of input. I really love those types of projects. It's a great feeling to know that I really helped shape the final design. It doesn't always happen like that!

In fact, the original design idea is often quite different to what is actually built. So I'd say that the key thing needed in all design projects is compromise. It's essential. I mean, even if you think your design is perfect, the client is likely to request certain changes. You have to incorporate those wishes into the design, regardless of your personal preferences.

Part 3
Audio track: B2_Listening_1_3.mp3

Part 3. You will hear five short extracts in which people are talking about a common topic. For questions 19 to 23, choose the best answer: A–H. Use the letters only once. There are three extra statements which are not attributed to a speaker.

You hear five people talking about eating out.

Speaker 1   Eating out with friends is such a sociable, fun thing to do, especially if the whole group orders different things to share. This doesn't have to be very expensive if you go when restaurants are running special deals. I'd describe myself as quite adventurous when it comes to eating out. I'm always looking for new places to try, and I tend to choose the things on the menu that I've never heard of, or things that seem a bit odd. I mean, what's the point of ordering the same things that you'd cook at home?

Speaker 2   Do you know the expression "your eyes are bigger than your belly"? Well, that's me, I'm afraid! I can't help ordering too much when I see all the exciting dishes on the menu. To be fair, some restaurants serve quite small portions, so I never know how much to order. But even so, I always end up with things that I can't finish. But restaurants are usually happy to wrap up whatever you can't finish so that you can take it away with you to finish later. That's great because I hate the idea of wasting food.

Speaker 3   I think famous TV chefs and social media trends have made eating out more popular nowadays than it used to be. You know, people want to try the latest food trends, or go to the coolest places to eat, don't they? But for me, eating out's something I can only afford to do for special occasions. I don't want to waste my time or money going somewhere I don't like. I might read restaurant reviews or ask friends for recommendations, but I usually stick to my favourite restaurants instead of going somewhere new.

Speaker 4   If it takes all night to get your food or if the staff are rude, it can spoil the experience of eating out. I've been going to the same place for years because all the staff make you feel really welcome. They don't have the best menu or prices in town, but nowhere else can match the quality of their service. I think some of the newer, trendy restaurants forget about the importance of this aspect.

Speaker 5   Don't get me wrong, I do like going to restaurants. As the person who makes all the family meals, it's a treat not having to cook once in a while! But it's not particularly relaxing, is it? Restaurants are either too crowded so you can't hear what anyone's

Cambridge B2 First Listening

saying, or they have seats that are too hard. It drives me crazy when they play music as well. Who wants that when they're having dinner? I don't know if it's just me, but I feel like I have to look smart when I eat out. I don't really like that, to be honest.

Part 4

Audio track: B2_Listening_1_4.mp3

Part 4. You hear an interview with a psychologist called Helen Simpson, who is talking about mindfulness. For questions 24 to 30, choose the best answer: A, B or C.

Interviewer	Hello, and welcome to the show. Today we're discussing one of the biggest lifestyle trends in recent years: mindfulness. I'm joined by psychologist Dr Helen Simpson who's written a book on the subject called *The Road to Mindfulness*. Welcome, Dr Simpson.
Speaker	Thank you.
Interviewer	Dr Simpson, I think many people are confused about the term 'mindfulness'. It's everywhere these days – I've even seen advertisements for 'mindfulness soap', whatever that means!
Speaker	Well, unfortunately, companies misuse the term to sell products. But actually, 'mindfulness' simply means feeling connected to what's happening around us. That might sound complicated, but in my book I show people how to apply simple mindfulness techniques to improve their lives.
Interviewer	It sounds like mindfulness is a way of thinking.
Speaker	Yes, exactly. Mindfulness helps us focus on the present, making us feel calmer. And it's something we need now more than ever. There's clear evidence that people's stress levels are increasing.
Interviewer	Oh dear! So what's causing that?
Speaker	Well, the main problem seems to be multi-tasking.
Interviewer	But isn't that supposed to be an efficient use of our time?
Speaker	That's what we assume. But when we have a conversation with a friend while checking our social media and thinking about work emails, we simply cannot focus. We just end up feeling under pressure.
Interviewer	And we achieve less when we're stressed.
Speaker	Yes, and don't forget the impact stress can have on our body too. But we also need to talk about mind-wandering.
Interviewer	Ah, yes, you mention that in your book. Could you explain what you mean?
Speaker	Not focusing on the current task because you're thinking about something else. And research conducted in the US suggests that mind-wandering actually has a negative impact on our happiness.
Interviewer	And talking about research, you've investigated mindfulness training in work environments, haven't you?
Speaker	That's right. Mindfulness is a subject that's discussed a lot at academic conferences. So although I'd heard about it in seminars, it didn't really attract my attention until I was having problems coping with my own work pressures.
Interviewer	OK, so I think the listeners would love to know what you mean by 'mindfulness training'.
Speaker	Well, it's about developing our ability to focus. We aim to direct our full attention to something and really notice things about that object, like sounds, sights and our own thoughts. Over time, we become better at focusing and being aware of our own feelings.

Interviewer	So can you give us an example of a mindfulness exercise you'd do with a client?
Speaker	Well, I'd start by asking them to do a simple task like washing some plates. I'd get them to concentrate on exactly how the water feels, what they can hear, and so on. And yes, the client feels a bit silly at first! But they soon relax and understand the purpose of the task. They start to see the value of just staying in the present moment.
Interviewer	Well, we're nearly out of time but do you have any other mindfulness tips?
Speaker	Well, things like drawing or painting are great for mindfulness, and any type of outdoor exercise is too. But there's something even simpler that anyone can do. The next time you're eating a meal, give it your full attention. Don't look at your phone or watch TV. Instead, really focus on what you're eating, how it tastes, how it looks, whether you're enjoying it. Everyone should give it a try. It's like eating for the very first time!
Interviewer	How interesting! Well, thank you Dr Simpson…

Test 2

Part 1
Audio track: B2_Listening_2_1.mp3

Part 1. You will hear people talking in eight different situations. For questions 1 to 8, you must choose the best answer: A, B or C.

Question 1 — **You hear two students talking about student life. What is the girl disappointed with?**

Speaker 1	I can't believe it's nearly the end of our first term already!
Speaker 2	Yes, I had no idea what I was letting myself in for!
Speaker 1	But you're enjoying your course so far, aren't you?
Speaker 2	Well, I've got no complaints about the subject, but maybe I should've picked a different college.
Speaker 1	The tutors are excellent.
Speaker 2	I know, but it's all the other stuff, isn't it? I mean, our accommodation's rubbish, there aren't many student clubs. And how come we don't even have a decent library? They didn't mention any of that on the open day!
Speaker 1	I think you're being a bit unfair. I love it here.

Question 2 — **You hear a woman talking about being a chef. What does she think has been the most important development in her industry?**

When I talk to young chefs, many of them are getting their initial inspiration from social media influencers and TV cooking shows. That wasn't really much of a thing when I was first training. Of course, anyone interested in a career as a chef still needs to get plenty of work experience in restaurant kitchens. But something nobody could've predicted is how popular vegetarian food has become. Nowadays, there are so many meat-free options in restaurants, which is wonderful to see. And there are so many

Cambridge B2 First Listening

plant-based products that we can use now instead of meat. This has completely transformed the restaurant scene and food industry.

Question 3 You hear an announcement at a supermarket. What is on sale for a special price at the moment?

Welcome to Freshmart where there's fantastic quality at unbeatable prices, week in, week out. New this week is our award-winning French cheese. If you want to try before you buy, head over to the stall by the bakery section for some free samples. And while you're there, why not pick up some delicious bread? There's 25% off all our loaves this week. They're perfect with salted butter and the sandwich filling of your choice…

Question 4 You hear part of a radio interview. What is the interviewer doing?

Speaker 1 Minister, your department has announced a £12 million initiative to encourage more pupils to study music.

Speaker 2 And when you consider that less than 3% of pupils currently have access to music lessons, this will have a tremendous impact. We aim to increase participation in music by 38%.

Speaker 1 But behind all those facts and figures, are you happy with this decision? Shouldn't this money be spent elsewhere?

Speaker 2 Well, given that our music industry is worth billions, we need to invest in the next generation of musical talent.

Speaker 1 So can you explain the decision to cut teacher salaries? The listeners would love to know your views.

Speaker 2 Well, I…

Question 5 You overhear two fans talking about their football club. How does the boy feel?

Speaker 1 Well, that wasn't a thrilling match, and at least we didn't lose. We should've won, though. We made too many mistakes near the end of the match.

Speaker 2 It's lack of fitness. That's down to the coach. And it's obvious the players don't understand his instructions.

Speaker 1 Well, he's definitely got a good eye for new players. He's managed to get Jack Martin and Roberto Lopez!

Speaker 1 Yes! I can't wait for them to start. They'll make a huge difference.

Speaker 2 If they adapt to our style of play. I'm not sure they'll fit in.

Speaker 1 We can't expect instant miracles, but we'll win cups with them in the long-term.

Question 6 Your cousin has left a voicemail message about a trip. What does your cousin want to do?

Thanks for sending me all those links about the guided tours and cooking classes we can do during the trip. We definitely won't get bored, will we? I know you'd like to arrange them now but we're not going in peak tourist season so I doubt they'll get fully booked. And actually, about that, I'm not sure about the Sun Hotel. Considering when

Transcripts

we're going, I think they're charging way over the standard rate. I'd be happier if we shopped around for a better deal. Is that OK with you?

Question 7 You overhear two people discussing a problem. What do they decide to do?

Speaker 1 Have you seen the mess outside number 34? Broken chairs, car parts, even an old sofa!

Speaker 2 It's so selfish. My grandmother's 93 with poor eyesight. She had to walk in the road this morning because all their rubbish was blocking the pathway.

Speaker 1 Should we go and talk to them? I'm sure they don't mean to be a nuisance.

Speaker 2 They're doing it on purpose – just because someone called the police about the loud music they were playing all night.

Speaker 1 We'll need to involve the council then. It's their responsibility to keep the streets clean and safe.

Speaker 2 That's true. If you call them and I email, they'll hopefully respond.

Speaker 1 OK.

Question 8 You hear an expert talking on the radio about antiques. What advice does he give the listeners?

People often want to know whether there's much profit to be made from buying and selling antiques. And there certainly is if you do your research. It's not necessarily about finding rare, valuable items. Even relatively mass-market, low-quality items can pay off if you know which market to target when you're selling them. For instance, people living in city apartments are less likely to want antique farming equipment, so it might be worth focusing on potential customers in rural locations. But other than that, if a simple object by an unknown producer appeals to you, don't worry about its value, just buy it and enjoy it!

Part 2

Audio track: B2_Listening_2_2.mp3

Part 2. You hear Carl Johnson, a company director, talking about his business. For questions 9 to 18, complete the sentences with a word or short phrase.

I'm the founder and director of a company which 8pecializes in drone photography. Basically, drones are remote-controlled robots with cameras which you can fly. This helps us to do photography from great heights – you know, aerial photography.

In the past, drones were only used for military purposes. For example, armies flew drones over jungles or forests when they were trying to detect people or objects because it was easier than trying to do that on foot.

But now, drone technology is also widely used in many different areas. As I said before, you can fly drones over land which is quite inaccessible. So, scientists use them to look for environmental changes over large areas.

But that's not all. Really, it's amazing what drones can do nowadays, and people are starting to see the commercial potential of drones. For instance, they're increasingly being used for creative purposes. All those overhead shots of beautiful landscapes or cities can be filmed using drones. In fact, most of our clients work in film production.

And I'm really excited about one of our latest projects which is in a completely different area. Two major agricultural corporations in the USA have just started using

Cambridge B2 First Listening

our drones to check what's happening with their crops, and to see which areas need more water or pest control. Of course, this could be done in other ways but the main benefit of using drones is that it saves so much time.

The expansion of my industry in recent years has been incredible, and I think that's mainly due to the falling price of basic drones. I suppose it's like all technology – as soon as it becomes affordable for the mass market, that's when it really takes off.

I've noticed a growing number of people flying drones in parks and on beaches just as a hobby. That's why my company is about to launch an online course to teach people the basics of how to use drones for photography and filming.

A market I hadn't considered until recently was social media. Many well-known online personalities want to make their content stand out. Being able to use drones can help these people film dramatic content that's bound to get a positive response.

But one thing I would say to anyone thinking of using drones is that it's essential to understand all the rules and laws concerning privacy. It's unacceptable to use drones to film areas that are protected by law. In fact, as drones become a more common sight, I expect more legislation to control their use. I'd definitely support that.

But apart from that, I can only see the sector developing further. Forgive the bad joke, but I really do think the sky's the limit for my company!

Part 3

Audio track: B2_Listening_2_3.mp3

Part 3. You will hear five short extracts in which people are talking about a common topic. For questions 19 to 23, choose the best answer: A–H. Use the letters only once. There are three extra statements which are not attributed to a speaker.

You hear five people talking about advertising.

Speaker 1 Nowadays, advertising isn't just limited to TV commercials, magazines or the billboards you see in streets or shopping centres. There are also all the advertisements you get when you're online, you know, the pop-ups. Now, I wouldn't say I like them, but I must admit, they do work. I mean, how many times are you searching for something online when suddenly, an advert appears for exactly the thing you've been looking for? I've definitely decided to buy stuff after seeing these adverts. But even so, it does make me worry about how much companies are monitoring what we're doing online.

Speaker 2 Some people find TV commercials amusing or entertaining, but I usually just find them annoying, especially when they interrupt my favourite TV shows. And anyway, you can't really believe anything they tell you in these adverts. I mean, I highly doubt that a top athlete would actually eat burgers or chocolates in real life, yet they happily promote them in commercials and act like they eat them all the time! I know there are laws about what companies are allowed to say in adverts so they're not allowed to lie directly, but I still think most advertisements bend the truth.

Speaker 3 We've been studying advertising at school recently, and it's been fascinating to learn about all the techniques companies use to make their advertising engaging. In fact, it's made me analyse the advertising messages I see all around me, and let's face it, there's so much advertising in daily life – it's everywhere! But now I have a better understanding of how advertising works, I think it would be a really interesting career, so I've decided to study marketing at college. I like the idea of finding ways to communicate ideas in a creative way to consumers.

Transcripts

Speaker 4 In my country, companies aren't allowed to use fake scientific information or make up statistics in their advertising, but I don't think the legislation goes far enough. It's not that the adverts are dishonest exactly, it's more that they make consumers feel bad about themselves. You know, they make people feel that they have to buy things that they don't actually need to feel better about a problem that doesn't really exist. I don't think that should be allowed. And I don't like the way companies target children either. There should be far more controls on the advertising shown during children's TV programmes.

Speaker 5 Love it or hate it, advertising has been a part of life for decades. You can tell how old someone is by the TV adverts they remember. And video-sharing sites are full of clips of old advertisements, because people love seeing the adverts they remember from their childhood. Personally, I think it's interesting to see the differences in advertising around the world. In my country, there's a lot of humour in our advertising, whereas in some places the same product might be advertised in a more serious way. So, from that perspective, I think adverts tell us a lot about a society's values and culture.

Part 4

Audio track: B2_Listening_2_4.mp3

Part 4. You hear an interview with a woman called Louise Harper, who works as hotel manager in Malta. For questions 24 to 30, choose the best answer: A, B or C.

Interviewer Welcome to the show. Today we're talking about tourism, and I'm joined by Louise Harper, manager of the Pine Star Hotel in Malta. Welcome, Louise. Maybe we could start by talking about your job?

Speaker Hi. I'm basically responsible for the entire hotel. I was specifically recruited to find ways to develop the business, like new services we could offer. That's my primary role. But of course, I'm always available to offer guidance to the staff, so that our guests get the best possible experience.

Interviewer And you moved from your home country to work in Malta, didn't you?

Speaker Well, I didn't actually have a specific job lined up. My parents are retired and live there now so my main motivation for moving was to be closer to them. They were always telling me how happy they were there, so it really wasn't a difficult decision to make!

Interviewer And I imagine Malta would have a lot of opportunities in the tourism sector?

Speaker Absolutely! Tourism has really taken off in Malta, so I knew there would be plenty of opportunities. It's incredible how much the sector has developed. That's great news for me as I have a lot of industry experience. There's no reason why I can't make the most of all the exciting opportunities for many years to come.

Interviewer That's great. Do you think tourism is changing generally?

Speaker Yes, without a doubt. For one thing, overseas travel is no longer restricted to the elite in society who only stay in five-star hotels. We've already seen a move away from that with the rise in cheaper city breaks. But I think the next big trend will be holidays with more emphasis on activities like extreme sports. Young people in particular want to have adventures and experiences, and that's the kind of thing they love to do.

Interviewer What's your take on green tourism? I mean, tourism designed to cause less environmental harm.

Speaker Ah yes, eco-tourism. Well look, unfortunately, a lot of people aren't really sure what it means. That's because there are some companies that use terms like 'green' or 'eco' just because they know it will attract more customers. But actually, true eco-tourism can be extremely beneficial. I think if hotels, tour operators and transport providers work together, they can make it possible for people to explore the world without

Cambridge B2 First Listening

	damaging the environment. At the same time, it can teach tourists the importance of being responsible too.
Interviewer	I see. And do you have any tips for our listeners about planning the perfect holiday?
Speaker	Well, it's often said you shouldn't travel during the height of the tourist season because it's so expensive. But let's be realistic: if you have school-age children, you can't travel during term time! What else? Well, there's no harm in reading what other travellers have posted on the internet about their experiences. That can be useful research, providing you don't rely solely on that. One thing I'd say is to not sign up for every single tour and trip. You might just feel like relaxing one day, so don't commit yourself to exhausting activities every day!
Interviewer	Great tips! And finally, Louise, what does the future hold for you? Will you be opening your own hotel chain?
Speaker	I think my strengths lie more in analysing the sector. So ultimately, I see myself offering advice to other travel companies. I could do that for clients all around the world, which is exciting. I like the idea of having a business that could take me to other places from time to time. After all, I love travelling!
Interviewer	Well, that sounds wonderful. Thank you, Louise…

Test 3

Part 1

Audio track: B2_Listening_3_1.mp3

Part 1. You will hear people talking in eight different situations. For questions 1 to 8, you must choose the best answer: A, B or C.

Question 1   You hear two colleagues talking about a work project. Which aspect of the project do they disagree about?

Speaker 1	I'm pleased about the design Rob selected. The architect's plans look amazing.
Speaker 2	Agreed, but I wonder who Rob will get to work on it. The people we used last time would be my preference.
Speaker 1	Yes, mine too. They were great. But I suspect we won't have such a large team this time. We really need to keep our costs down.
Speaker 2	But if we try to do this on the cheap, the end result won't be as good.
Speaker 1	Well, we don't need to invest such a large sum this time. It's a pretty straightforward project.
Speaker 2	I'm not convinced. There are always unexpected costs to consider.
Speaker 1	Well, let's see.

Question 2   You overhear a woman leaving a voicemail about a shopping trip. How did she feel during the trip?

Hi mum, I'm just on my way back. I can see how people get carried away at wedding shows – there's so much choice! But I'm glad you warned me about how much people

Transcripts

charge at these events! I managed to find a lot of things that would be perfect for the wedding party. And I took your advice – I tried to negotiate for low prices. But I wish you'd been with me – you're so much better at it than I am! I felt really uncomfortable. Anyway, call me back and I'll tell you more about it.

Question 3   **You overhear a conversation between two gym employees. What are the speakers complaining about?**

Speaker 1   Why are they taking the weights and exercise mats out of the fitness studio?

Speaker 2   There aren't enough in the training area.

Speaker 1   But what about Tom's circuit class? That starts in 15 minutes. And he'll need them for the dumbbell class too.

Speaker 2   Haven't you heard? Tom's called in sick. So, no classes are running this evening.

Speaker 1   Couldn't they find another instructor?

Speaker 2   No, the manager isn't willing to pay for a replacement. And of course, *we'll* be the ones dealing with angry clients.

Speaker 1   Well, for the amount this place charges, I'd complain too. I mean, the fancy showers and beautiful changing rooms don't make up for poor service.

Speaker 1   Exactly.

Question 4   **You overhear a conversation between two neighbours. What does the woman want her neighbour to do for her event?**

Speaker 1   Hi Anna, Maria told me you're planning an event to raise money for the hospital. What a great idea!

Speaker 2   Thanks, Mark. Yes, it's just a simple bake sale. People can make cakes, biscuits or whatever for us to sell. Actually, I was wondering if you'd be able to take part?

Speaker 1   Well, I'm not the world's best cook, but I'm sure I could manage a few biscuits.

Speaker 2   Fantastic. I've posted about it on Facebook and already received a few promises of financial support. I hadn't realised it was such an effective way to promote good causes.

Speaker 1   Well done! You're off to a great start.

Question 5   **You overhear a woman leaving a voicemail about a business meeting. What does the woman say about the meeting?**

Hi Ed, it's Miriam. Just to give you a quick update on the meeting we had with the accounting firm. Well, they're a friendly bunch and looked after us well. But the manager, Phil Barton, was pretty disorganised. He hadn't realised our meeting was today so he didn't have any notes with him, and he had to leave after 15 minutes. Fortunately, the rest of the team were there. They gave us a lot of very useful information about the project so it was worth going. I'll email you my notes when I get back to the office. Bye.

Question 6   **You hear a radio presenter talking about a film. What is the presenter doing?**

Now, can you believe it's been 30 years since the landmark film 'The House of Shadows' was released? Like many other people, I remember thinking the film was

Cambridge B2 First Listening

absolutely ground-breaking at the time with its plot about a superhero ghost. Since then, of course, there have been several films telling similar stories. So, now it's over to you. Tell us your memories of the 'The House of Shadows'. Do you think it's still an important piece of cinema? Text or call us now!

Question 7   You overhear two friends discussing a book. What do they agree about?

Speaker 1   Oh, you're reading the new Mo Harper novel! How are you finding it? It's funny but have you read his last one, *Red Shoe*? That's my personal favourite.

Speaker 2   I didn't know you liked Mo Harper! Most people have never even heard of him!

Speaker 1   Really? He's becoming quite fashionable. He's been on TV recently. It won't be long before he's really famous.

Speaker 2   Mo Harper? No way! But, you're right – the latest one's not quite as good as *Red Shoe*. But he definitely knows how to write great characters, doesn't he?

Speaker 1   I'm more into the exciting plots that keep you guessing. That's what he's best at for me.

Question 8   You hear a man speaking on a telephone. What is he trying to do?

Oh hello, I'm calling about the tickets I booked for the show on July 15th. … Mr Jack Smith. … Uh-huh. Yes, that's right, the credit card ending 6745. And I need to swap the booking for the July 16th performance instead. … No, I don't want my money back; can't you just transfer my tickets from the Thursday show to the Friday performance? … Yes, same seats if they're available please. … OK, so to confirm, my account won't be charged twice, will it? … Yes, I'll collect the tickets from the theatre, thanks.

Part 2

Audio track: B2_Listening_3_2.mp3

Part 2. You hear a radio presenter giving information about a film festival. For questions 9 to 18, complete the sentences with a word or short phrase.

Welcome to the show, and today's programme is about a subject very close to my heart because we're going to be talking about the wonderful Gleinston Film Festival. This event is in its fifteenth year now and is a highlight of the cultural calendar. And I'm not just saying that because it was founded by a cinema critic like me!

Although it has become known for its impressive range of international films, the festival was first intended as a way of promoting independent cinema. The founder, Jim Simpson, wanted to highlight that filmmaking shouldn't have to depend on major Hollywood production companies.

There are various award competitions during the festival, but not all films can be considered for the competitions. There are strict rules that filmmakers have to obey for their work to be selected. For instance, in keeping with the spirit of the festival, there are tight limits on the budgets of all competition films.

And along with all the usual things like awards for best science-fiction film or best drama, I'm personally delighted about the inclusion of a new category at this year's festival. For the first time, there's going to be a separate award for best animation film.

Transcripts

And regular listeners of this show will know how much I love that film genre!

Of course, gaining recognition in one of the competitions generates a lot of important publicity for filmmakers. That's particularly true for films competing for the Golden Heart award. Unlike the other competitions which are judged by a panel of film experts, this prize is determined by votes from the general public. So come along and let your opinions count!

But it's about more than just giving out awards. One of the other key principles at the festival is about education. That's why all the films that are shown have been chosen because they have a positive social impact in some way. For instance, they might cover important themes that aren't usually discussed by filmmakers, or their production helped the local community. Isn't that wonderful?

And this isn't just about the films themselves. As the festival has grown, it's of course attracted more commercial interest. Now, the committee wanted to ensure that the Festival remains committed to doing good. So I'm really impressed with their sponsorship policy – they only agree to partner with ethical companies, which I think is a great idea.

On top of that, all profits made by the festival go to good causes. For instance, a share goes to supporting film schools in the local areas. So who knows? Maybe the next international film star will be discovered after getting this financial support!

But if that all makes the festival sound very serious, then don't worry. This is one of the most relaxed and friendly events you can go to. In fact, as I always tell people, there's no other film festival that has such an enjoyable atmosphere. There's something for everyone, from the most enthusiastic of film fanatics to the casual viewer.

And another reason for the festival's appeal is that because it's still a relatively small event, there is far more interaction between festival participants. What I mean is that visitors have far more chances to meet the performers, which is something that doesn't happen at most other film festivals.

Well, I think I've spoken for long enough about this. Now it's time to meet one of this year's organisers…

Part 3

Audio track: B2_Listening_3_3.mp3

Part 3. You will hear five short extracts in which people are talking about a common topic. For questions 19 to 23, choose the best answer: A–H. Use the letters only once. There are three extra statements which are not attributed to a speaker.

You hear five people talking about school trips.

Speaker 1   I went on a five-day school geography trip to some Scottish islands when I was about sixteen. It was something to do with studying rocks … I think! It was interesting to see a different side to our teachers. You know, they were a bit more relaxed but it was strange seeing them dressed casually rather than in their normal work clothes! One thing I hadn't expected was that I'd miss my parents so much. And I couldn't wait to get home and sleep in my own bedroom. I suppose that's normal, because it was my first time being away from home.

Speaker 2   School trips must be an absolute nightmare for teachers! All those excited kids wandering off. I remember one class trip to a nature reserve. The teacher was going on and on about all the rules that we had to follow. Well, of course, my friend and I weren't paying much attention. We thought we had to return to the coach at 5pm, but actually we should have gone back at 4pm. Well, you can imagine how furious the teacher and the rest of the class were when we turned up an hour late. As a punishment, we weren't allowed to go on the next school trip.

Cambridge B2 First Listening

Speaker 3 We didn't do many class trips when I was at school, but they were definitely a highlight. Having the chance to get out of the classroom was so exciting to me, and I used to look forward to school trips for weeks beforehand. I even enjoyed the tasks they gave us to do on the trip, like taking notes on objects in a museum or identifying trees in a forest. Is there a better way to learn about something than actually seeing it with your own eyes? And it's even more fun when you get to spend time with your schoolfriends in a new place.

Speaker 4 Don't get me wrong, I liked it when our class used to go out on excursions, even if it was just to an art gallery. But I honestly don't know if I really learnt much on any of these trips. For example, I remember going on one trip to the coast where we were supposed to be collecting information about seabirds, but all I remember was spending the morning eating ice-cream and going into souvenir shops! I'm convinced there are more effective ways to learn, but still, I'm not complaining!

Speaker 5 In general, I'm in favour of school trips, but it depends on the type of activity the school organises. Some of the trips my school used to offer were far too expensive. I couldn't afford to go on all of the excursions, unfortunately. And to be honest, I didn't used to like the ones where we had to do a lot of physical activity, you know, like hiking. My favourite trips were the ones where we could watch a play or go to an art gallery. Those cultural experiences inspired me far more.

Part 4

Audio track: B2_Listening_3_4.mp3

Part 4. You hear an interview with a man called Rob Jackson, who works in the car industry. For questions 24 to 30, choose the best answer: A, B or C.

Interviewer Today, we're talking about electric vehicles. Electric vehicles are still relatively new, but today's guest, Rob Jackson, hopes that more of us will be using them soon. Welcome, Rob!

Speaker Thanks, lovely to be here.

Interviewer So Rob, you work for one of the largest electric car companies in America, don't you?

Speaker Well, the company is American, but we do business in many other places too. In fact, our vehicles sell faster in Europe than anywhere else, and sales are also taking off in Asia, which is very exciting.

Interviewer Okay – what's the difference between plug-in and hybrid-electric vehicles?

Speaker Basically, a plug-in electric vehicle runs entirely on electricity. You plug it in to charge it, just like your phone. Because they don't run on petrol or diesel, they don't cause harmful emissions. For that reason, they're much better for the environment. Hybrid-electric vehicles run mainly on a traditional diesel or petrol engine but also have an electric battery. While they are certainly better for the environment than traditional cars, we can't really compare them with electric vehicles.

Interviewer But hybrids are quite popular now, aren't they?

Speaker And that worries me. I wouldn't want people to buy them thinking they're as green as electric vehicles when they're not.

Interviewer Could you tell us about your work?

Speaker Well, I work as a lead engineer, responsible for vehicle optimisation. This simply means I look for ways to improve our vehicles.

Interviewer So you get to decide how the final product looks?

Speaker Not really! I focus on the technical side, specifically improving battery life. This makes

Transcripts

	it possible to travel further before re-charging. It's one of the main features we mention in our advertising.
Interviewer	At the moment, what sort of consumer is buying electric vehicles? I mean, are they practical for families?
Speaker	Oh, yes, absolutely, and that sector's going to become crucial as the market develops. But currently, my company does more business with young professionals. Our customers live and work in cities and rarely drive long distances. You don't see so many older people in rural areas using electric vehicles, but I'd love to change that.
Interviewer	But electric vehicles are still beyond the financial reach of a lot of people, aren't they? Many people would love to own one because they're far better for the environment, but they're too expensive.
Speaker	Well, the prices are definitely coming down. And actually, our research suggests the main reason people hesitate about buying electric vehicles is they're concerned about charging them. Unless these facilities are easily available to motorists, people won't buy electric vehicles.
Interviewer	And you mentioned research. Are you personally involved in that?
Speaker	Oh, yes. Research helps us find out what consumers think and helps improve our products. For instance, I was involved in a major study about how electric vehicles perform in different climates. We discovered that they consume more energy in colder temperatures. I'm now looking at the impact of car-sharing apps. These services make it possible to rent an electric vehicle with just one swipe of a phone. I'm collecting a lot of useful data about that.
Interviewer	Well, it sounds fascinating. You must enjoy your work.
Speaker	Yes, definitely! I've been an engineer for many years, working with many excellent companies. I've been fortunate enough to work all over the world, but I think my current role's perfect for me. I'm passionate about electric vehicles, and because it's a relatively new sector, there's still so much to discover. That's what I find so motivating and enjoyable about my work. Like most people, I value that above a top salary and company bonuses.
Interviewer	Well, thank you for joining us today, Rob…

Test 4

Part 1

Audio track: B2_Listening_4_1.mp3

Part 1. You will hear people talking in eight different situations. For questions 1 to 8, you must choose the best answer: A, B or C.

Question 1 You hear two people talking about a restaurant meal. Why is the woman annoyed?

Speaker 1	Well, that wasn't the best dining experience, was it?
Speaker 2	I know, and I'm sorry I didn't check the time of the reservation. I was convinced it was for quarter to seven, not half six.
Speaker 1	Even if you'd been on time, it wouldn't have made a difference. I mean, there was no record of our booking on the restaurant's computer system. I can't understand why it

Cambridge B2 First Listening

was cancelled without the restaurant telling us.

Speaker 2 Well, at least they gave us free desserts to apologise.

Speaker 1 Yes, but we didn't get seated for forty minutes, and that was their fault completely.

Question 2 **You hear a woman talking about leisure activities. Which activity does she feel she has benefitted from the most?**

There are lots of great activities to do in my town. My friend recommended joining her community choir. I'm not the world's best singer, but it's so much fun! And I've also joined an indoor climbing club. It was extremely hard at first, but I'm slowly improving. And I've noticed how much fitter and stronger I am now. For example, gardening tasks that used to make me out of breath are much easier now. I'd thoroughly recommend it.

Question 3 **You overhear a conversation in a shop. What does the customer tell the shop assistant?**

Speaker 1 Excuse me. Can I return online purchases to your store for a refund? I'd like to return this lamp, please.

Speaker 2 Of course. Is there anything wrong with it?

Speaker 1 Well, when it arrived, it looked smaller than I'd expected and not as nice. I ordered it two weeks ago, so it's still within the time limit, isn't it?

Speaker 2 That's right. You can return any item within one month of your purchase, providing you have proof of purchase.

Speaker 1 I've searched everywhere for it, but I don't know where I've put it.

Speaker 2 Well, if you have an email confirmation on your phone, you can use that.

Question 4 **You hear a woman presenting on a TV show. What is she talking about?**

Now, have you seen this vegetable in your supermarket? It looks like a big white carrot, but it's called a daikon. Daikons are very popular in Japan, and have a mild pepper taste that's sweeter than you might expect. They can be cooked, pickled and eaten raw. The skin's very thin so there's no need to peel it. Just wash it and you're ready to fry it or roast it, or add it to a lovely crunchy salad. And later, don't miss our wonderful daikon curry recipe. Don't worry if you can't find daikon in your local shops as we'll explain what you can use instead.

Question 5 **You hear two businesspeople talking about a work project. How does the man feel?**

Speaker 1 I'm so glad you're going to be part of the team working on Ed's project!

Speaker 2 Well, it took a lot persuasion to get me to agree. You know I'd already expressed reservations about the whole thing.

Speaker 1 Well, Ed always gets his way – he's a great negotiator!

Speaker 2 I suppose, but I haven't signed a contract yet, so let's wait and see. I can't quite believe the project's even happening. I'm half expecting them to announce that it's been cancelled due to lack of finance or something.

Speaker 1   Don't worry about that. If anything, I think you'll be impressed with the budget Ed's allocated.

Question 6   **You hear a sports commentary on the radio. What is the reporter doing?**

Some people were wondering whether Greencaster supporters would even turn up for this game, and who could blame them? And, as I look around the half-full stadium, there's no denying recent news stories have had an impact. Nobody's singing, and many fans are holding signs demanding the club management resigns. The overall feeling is that Greencaster Rovers is a club in crisis. Rovers surely need a good start to give their fans something to cheer about, otherwise, this is going to be very hard. And let's not forget, if Rovers lose, they're out of the cup. Will supporters get behind their team?

Question 7   **You overhear two friends talking about a hair salon. What does Marco's Salon regularly do?**

Speaker 1   I'm thinking of trying that new salon on Parker Street. I'm getting fed up with Marco's.

Speaker 2   Really? The staff at Marco's really know their stuff.

Speaker 1   Oh, I've got nothing against the quality of their work.

Speaker 2   So what's the issue? Have they put up their prices again?

Speaker 2   No, but it's all the upselling they do now. You know, you go in for just a haircut, and they encourage you to buy their fancy haircare range. Or push you to have some extra hair treatment.

Speaker 1   Oh, tell me about it! I came out of there last time with bottles of stuff I'll never use.

Speaker 2   Exactly.

Question 8   **You hear a conversation between two friends talking about a college open day. What course has the girl chosen?**

Speaker 1   That open day was so useful. I was really impressed by the range of science courses they offer.

Speaker 2   Me too. And did you see that demonstration by the engineering department? It was so cool!

Speaker 1   With the robots? Yes, I knew you'd like that! So, do you think you'll apply?

Speaker 2   Probably. What about you?

Speaker 1   Well, I went to the open day specifically to find out more about their faculty of medicine, but actually, the course that really stood out was biology. It's the right programme for me. I'm going to submit my application tomorrow.

Speaker 2   Great!

Cambridge B2 First Listening

Part 2
Audio track: B2_Listening_4_2.mp3

Part 2. You hear Donna Jackson, a professor, giving a lecture about the Hippocratic Oath. For questions 9 to 18, complete the sentences with a word or short phrase.

Good afternoon, everyone. I'll start by introducing myself. I'm Professor Donna Jackson. Unlike other professors in our faculty who are involved in researching diseases, my main role focuses on training new doctors. So, we'll be seeing each other a lot during your degree!

Now, today's lecture is about something called the Hippocratic Oath, and how as doctors we should be treating our patients. But you're not just going to sit and take notes during this session. I'm going to ask you to take part in some drama activities because they can really help you understand your patients' needs.

But first, I'd like to give you some background information. As I've just said, this session is about how we treat patients. What I'm talking about is how healthcare professionals behave with their patients. And obviously, a key part of that is that healthcare professionals – whatever their specific role – have to respect their patients. This is vital.

And this concept has been the foundation of healthcare for an extremely long time. In fact, we can go all the way back to Ancient Greece, which is when the Hippocratic Oath was developed. This oath, whose name comes from the Greek doctor Hippocrates, is a sort of moral code that sets out the key principles that doctors should follow when taking care of patients.

For centuries, medical schools and universities have asked doctors to swear by this oath. This basically means doctors have to promise to obey it. However, the Hippocratic Oath is no longer compulsory in the majority of medical schools. This is because modern alternatives and official guidelines are used instead. But the basic principles of the Oath shouldn't be forgotten.

So, let's talk about some of these principles. I'm sure you've heard of one of the most famous concepts associated with the Oath – the concept that doctors must 'do no harm'. This is a well-known phrase, but interestingly, these exact words didn't actually appear in the original Hippocratic Oath text. They appeared in much later translations of the Oath.

But what does this principle mean? Well, for me it's about accepting our limitations as medical professionals. When we're faced with difficult cases, we must be willing to consult more experienced colleagues rather than assuming that we can find the answer by ourselves. That's why I strongly believe every part of the healthcare system needs to prioritise teamwork. It's a key part of our profession.

And when I refer to healthcare systems, I include everyone who is involved in helping patients at any stage. And if we want an effective healthcare system, we have to start with good communication. Putting that in place enables all the people involved in patient care to do their work in the right way. This principle was mentioned in the Hippocratic Oath, and has been developed in modern guidelines.

As the Hippocratic Oath recognised almost two thousand years ago, our work carries a great deal of responsibility. As medical professionals, we have to be able to justify all the key decisions we take. That's why there are so many official procedures in place nowadays.

So really, while the Hippocratic Oath itself is an ancient document which may seem outdated to us now, it was the foundation which led to the development of modern medicine. Obviously, all medical guidelines are a reflection of the values of a society. So as societies change, so too do the specific rules we need to follow as medical professionals, even if the basic principles remain the same.

So now, let's look at these ideas in more detail…

Transcripts

Part 3
Audio track: B2_Listening_4_3.mp3

Part 3. You will hear five short extracts in which people are talking about a common topic. For questions 19 to 23, choose the best answer: A–H. Use the letters only once. There are three extra statements which are not attributed to a speaker.

You hear five people talking about their use of social media.

Speaker 1 When it comes to new technology or trends, I'm not what you'd call an early adopter. I tend to wait and see if something is going to catch on properly or if it's just a short-term fad. I was probably the last person in my social circle to start using social media. At first, I didn't really see why people would want to share so much about their lives all the time, but I've realised that it's actually quite useful. For me, it's a practical way to give quick updates when I can't be bothered to get in touch with people individually.

Speaker 2 I know everyone says it, but social media really does open up a world of social opportunities. I mean, you can use it to find other people who are into the same things. That's what I do. In my hometown, I don't know many people into things like graphic novels, but through social media I've met all sorts of people who feel the same way I do about comic books. Well, I say 'meet', but of course I haven't spent any time with them in real life, but you never know, I might one day. But even if I don't, I still consider them my friends in one sense.

Speaker 3 Social media isn't just about posting photos and sharing videos of cats, you know! I mean, personally, social media has taught me so much about what's happening in the world, people's problems and subjects that don't get enough attention on the news. I mean, if you think about it, social media is really a reflection of our daily lives and what matters to us, isn't it? So, it's the perfect place to share opinions about important topics. If it hadn't been for people sharing things on their newsfeeds, I doubt I'd know much about deforestation, for example.

Speaker 4 I'm the type of person that can spend hours scrolling through my feed, clicking 'like' on everything and reading utter nonsense. I don't think social media is a problem in itself, but I was starting to feel like if I wasn't on it all the time, I was missing out. That was starting to make me feel anxious, which is when I realised I needed to cut down my usage. I still use it but I now set strict time limits. I think I've got the balance right. I'm much happier not being glued to my phone the whole time.

Speaker 5 Is it just me that's sick of seeing fake selfies on social media? I mean, people use so many filters to look perfect, but it's so boring! And anyway, we all know those filters are fake, so why bother? But all this fake content can be harmful for younger social media users. What if they see all these images and want to copy them, not realising that they're all fake? I've seen people younger than 10 becoming obsessed with how they look, and that's wrong. As for me, I sometimes share selfies to capture a fun moment in time, but not because I think I'm a top model!

Cambridge B2 First Listening

Part 4

Audio track: B2_Listening_4_4.mp3

Part 4. You hear an interview with a consumer expert called Nigel Wilkins, who is talking about money. For questions 24 to 30, choose the best answer: A, B or C.

Interviewer Hello everyone – welcome to the programme. Joining me today is Nigel Wilkins, star of the TV show 'Money Matters'. Welcome Nigel, and congratulations on making such an entertaining and informative programme. I often watch it with my kids who are 14 and 16. We love it!

Speaker Thank you! It's very satisfying to know that families are watching it together. And a lot of schools contact me saying they use it in their classes to teach students about financial subjects, which is fantastic. We really hoped to reach that age group – you know, students who will be young adults in just a few years.

Interviewer So, what's the secret of the programme's success?

Speaker Well, 'Money Matters' isn't unique in terms of the subjects we cover. But what makes us stand out is our approach to the content. We discuss important topics, yes, but we still manage to make it fun. And viewer feedback suggests we've got the right balance – they're not shy about telling us what they like and don't like about the programme!

Interviewer Well, the programme certainly does a great job of raising awareness of important subjects. But I wondered what you think about the pressures on teenagers nowadays?

Speaker Yes, well, companies are definitely targeting young consumers now – encouraging them to spend too much.

Interviewer Especially since their video games and smartphone apps are full of advertising!

Speaker Yes. And at the same time, banks are offering young people credit cards too easily. That's why it's essential to educate young people about financial literacy. This simply means basic financial matters such as debt, interest rates and savings. I'd like the government to introduce this subject into schools.

Interviewer So, do you think attitudes to saving and spending have changed in recent years?

Speaker Definitely! I think it's largely due to celebrity culture. Stars share their lives online, and many of them are paid to promote designer goods, and so on. So, this lifestyle seems more accessible. At the same time, credit card companies are really pushing the message of 'buy now, pay later'. In the past, when you couldn't afford something, you'd save up until you had enough money. But that's changed.

Interviewer You don't sound very happy about this, Nigel.

Speaker Well, I just think this constant consumption's going too far. My worry is we're forgetting to appreciate what we already have. If we're constantly buying things, everything loses its value. We just replace things whenever something newer comes along. What does that say about us as a society? And it's such a waste of our natural resources.

Interviewer But there are also more sustainable forms of consumption, aren't there?

Speaker Yes, for instance, there's growing interest in second-hand products, and items that have been produced using recycled materials. Similarly, people are swapping items they no longer use with other people. And you might remember the programme I did a few weeks ago about repair cafés? People are taking their broken objects to these businesses to learn how to fix them. So yes, there is hope.

Interviewer So, what's next for you Nigel? The listeners would love you to confirm if there'll be another series of 'Money Matters'!

Speaker Well, we're in discussions so let's wait and see. But it wouldn't be until next year because I'm just about to start writing my first novel. I wanted to write something that kids could read and enjoy.

Interviewer Oh, how exciting! But with everything we've talked about today, wouldn't you fancy getting involved in policy-making or campaigning? Maybe even working in

Transcripts

	government? I'm sure you'd get a lot of public support.
Speaker	I don't think that's for me.
Interviewer	Fair enough! Well, thanks for joining us today, Nigel.
Speaker	My pleasure!

Test 5

Part 1

Audio track: B2_Listening_5_1.mp3

Part 1. You will hear people talking in eight different situations. For questions 1 to 8, you must choose the best answer: A, B or C.

Question 1 — You hear two people talking about their favourite football team. What does the girl say is the team's main strength?

Speaker 1	You know what? I'm convinced Rovers are going to do well this season.
Speaker 2	Well, you say that every year! We still need a decent goalkeeper for our weak defence.
Speaker 1	Don't be so negative! A few mistakes are to be expected with the way we play. We're much better going forward – it's what we do best. Look at how many goals we scored last season.
Speaker 2	Yes, but we need more experienced players. The team tries its best, but they can't maintain it for the whole season.
Speaker 1	Well, I think we've got the perfect players for the fast, energetic way Rovers have always played.

Question 2 — You hear a woman talking about travelling with friends. What does she think is the most useful piece of advice?

Going on holiday with friends can be amazing. But before you go, talk about your expectations of the holiday. For example, decide which expenses you'll share as a group. Also, remember that everyone enjoys doing different things on holiday, whether it's relaxing on a beach, going hiking or visiting museums. It's almost impossible to find the perfect activity that'll please everyone. Instead, it's well worth including opportunities for everyone to do their own thing. That's the main thing I'd recommend for an enjoyable group holiday because, after following your own interests, you'll be excited about seeing each other and sharing stories about your adventures.

Question 3 — You hear an announcement at a concert venue. What problem is being explained?

Ladies and gentlemen, major travel delays across the transport network this evening have affected tonight's performance.

Cambridge B2 First Listening

As performances are not allowed to continue past 10:30pm in order to comply with local laws, we have taken the difficult decision that tonight's performance cannot go ahead.

You will of course receive a full refund from the ticket office, and please accept a free drink and snack in our café as our apology for the inconvenience.

Question 4   **You hear a woman talking on a TV show. What is she talking about?**

The themes explored in 'The White Elephant' are quite unlike anything Max Spielman has covered in his previous work. Gone are Spielman's complex plots and poetic scripts. Instead, in this adaptation of Lisa Stanley's best-selling novel, it's the main character that shines. Archie is a bus driver whose ordinary life changes after one random event. The character is brought to life on screen by Adam Miller, making his cinematic debut. Overall, I'd definitely recommend 'The White Elephant'.

Question 5   **You hear two band members talking about their new singer. How does the woman feel?**

Speaker 1   I'm so glad Lauren's agreed to join the band, she's got such a unique voice.

Speaker 2   Yes, she brings something fresh to our songs.

Speaker 1   And now I can't wait to get into the studio and start working on some new music. I hope Lauren's ready for that.

Speaker 2   Well, I don't think she's written many of her own songs before, but it would be great to encourage her. I'm sure she can contribute a lot.

Speaker 1   Yes, and she seems just as excited as we are. She's already started making suggestions about concert venues, so I'm glad she's committed to the band.

Question 6   **You hear two people at a social event. What is the woman doing?**

Speaker 1   It's Amy Jackson, isn't it? I'm Ed, I work with Lucy at the bank.

Speaker 2   Nice to meet you Ed, yes Lucy said you would be at this event today.

Speaker 1   Actually, I'm looking for a new marketing manager and Lucy told me you'd be perfect as you've worked in the banking sector.

Speaker 2   Thanks for keeping me in mind but I'm not looking for a new position at present.

Speaker 1   Well, here's my business card. Do think about it.

Speaker 2   Thanks, I don't think it's the right role for me. But I can certainly suggest some other people you might want to contact.

Question 7   **You overhear a husband and wife who have just come back from a holiday. What do they agree on?**

Speaker 1   Just think; this time yesterday we were on a tropical island! A week just wasn't long enough, was it?

Speaker 2   Definitely not! Next time I'd go for longer and spend more time actually relaxing. And I'd stay in a different hotel.

Transcripts

Speaker 1   Mmm. Good point. I mean, the one we stayed in was alright, but for the price they charged, I was expecting something nicer.

Speaker 2   Me too. But other than that, I thought everything else on the island was quite reasonable. The restaurants were great value.

Speaker 1   Well, I wouldn't say they were cheap but they were excellent.

Question 8   **You hear a trainer talking to a client at the gym. What is he trying to do?**

OK, Dan, if you want to be able to lift heavier weights, you've got to work on your technique. You're just using your arms and shoulders, and that's why you're getting tired quickly. Remember to use the strength and power in your legs. Let's try it again. Move down into a squat position, and then, as you move back up to standing, use that power to help you lift the weight up above your head. And try not to lean over so much, your body position is too bent, so you're putting strain on your knees. That's it, yes. That's looking much better now.

Part 2

Audio track: B2_Listening_5_2.mp3

Part 2. You hear Julia Richards, a local official, giving a presentation about the proposed development of a new business park. For questions 9 to 18, complete the sentences with a word or short phrase.

Thank you for coming today. My name's Julia Richards and I'm here to update you on the latest developments regarding the construction of the new business park in our town. I'm sure you'll agree it's an exciting project which could potentially lead to better employment opportunities in our local area.

And on that subject, let me remind you that, as well as all the office buildings, the business park will also include a cutting-edge media centre. We hope this will attract leading companies in many different sectors. And we're confident that the business park will be especially important for companies in the IT sector.

In fact, if our projections are correct, we won't have to wait long until our hard work and investment will pay off. Within just five years, I'm sure that the entire community will be able to see the economic benefits of the business park. This is why I'm convinced that this project is the right one for our town.

And I also wanted to reassure everyone that the entire team behind the project are firmly committed to building the business park in a way that minimises any possible environmental damage. For instance, I'm relieved that the project managers are taking measures to protect wildlife in the local area.

But it's not just about trying to prevent any negative impacts during the construction phase. This business park will actually make a positive contribution to the environment. The installation of solar panels on the site will mean that it will be possible to generate significant amounts of solar power, something which will benefit the whole town.

So, hopefully I've managed to address many of the concerns you may have about this project. But I'd like to talk about some of the negative publicity the project has been attracting recently. I'm aware that some people aren't happy about the project, and I want to address some of the things that have been mentioned in the media recently.

First of all, disruption to local residents. Now, I know many people are concerned about the fact that constructing such a large business park will cause a lot of disruption in the local area in terms of road closures, noise and so on. However, I want to make it clear that there will be less disruption than has been reported in the media. Most of the building work will be on the west side of the site, far away from

Cambridge B2 First Listening

residential areas.

I'm also aware that people are concerned that the business park will mean increased traffic. I agree that we don't want more cars in the area, which is why it's so important for people using the business park to have alternative ways to reach the site. That's why I'm campaigning very actively at the moment for better public transport options that will encourage people to use buses or trains rather than drive.

But of course, my campaign will only succeed if we can convince the local council that the demand for such links is high enough to be worth the investment. And this is why I need your help. I'm asking for volunteers who can help me collect data from local residents and business owners. If you'd like to be involved, please come and talk to me after the presentation.

And that brings me to my final point. I hope I've highlighted the positives that the business park will bring. But really, the business park depends on the support of the people who live in the local area – people like you. You are in an ideal position to improve the project so that the business park will be a success for everyone. So now, if you have any questions…

Part 3

Audio track: B2_Listening_5_3.mp3

Part 3. You will hear five short extracts in which people are talking about a common topic. For questions 19 to 23, choose the best answer: A–H. Use the letters only once. There are three extra statements which are not attributed to a speaker.

You hear five people talking about their hobbies.

Speaker 1 Most of my hobbies are sports-related. I play basketball for a local team, and then I'm also a member of a volleyball club. And whenever I'm free at the weekend I play tennis. My friends are all members of the same sports clubs and teams, and I'm not sure I would have signed up for so many activities if they hadn't invited me along in the first place! I think playing sport has really boosted my self-esteem. You know, I'm less shy now and I feel good about myself because I can see that I'm improving and getting fitter.

Speaker 2 To be honest, I'm not really sure I have any hobbies, unless you count things like checking social media or watching TV! I mean, I do go out with friends when I can, but it's rare for me to have free time. And even when I do meet up with friends, we don't really 'do' anything – we just hang out. I'd love to take up an actual hobby – you know, like learning to dance –but there's no way I can commit to anything that involves going to classes or regular practice. At the moment, my crazy work schedule makes that virtually impossible.

Speaker 3 Oh, I've had lots of interesting hobbies. Skateboarding, salsa dancing, knitting, jewellery making – you name it, I've tried it! But I'll hold my hands up and admit that I never really stick to any of my hobbies for long. I'm really enthusiastic about them at first, but I soon lose interest so then it's on to the next thing. I don't know why I do that, but I suppose I just have a short attention span. But anyway, I like having variety in my life. Why limit yourself to one pastime when there are so many fun things to try?

Speaker 4 Whenever I meet someone for the first time and they ask 'What are you into?', I love seeing their reaction when I tell them. Nine times out of ten, people are surprised or curious when they find out I'm into curling. In fact, I often have to explain what curling is. It's a team sport played on ice, and it's all about strategy. I grew up in Scotland where it's quite popular, but hardly anyone plays it here in England. I had to travel back to Scotland to play. I was really pleased when I finally found a small curling club in England, about an hour away. I manage to play a few times a month.

Transcripts

Speaker 5   Everyone complains they're too busy for hobbies. I know what they mean, but it's really important to make time to develop your own interests. We all need time just doing the things that make us happy. That's why I'm getting back into photography. It's something I used to love doing at university. But then after I graduated, I focused on work, family, all that, and gradually stopped taking photos. But I went to a photography exhibition recently and it made me really miss my old hobby. I signed up for a course to refresh my skills and now I love photography even more than ever!

Part 4

Audio track: B2_Listening_5_4.mp3

Part 4. You hear an interview with a scientist called Mark Richards, who studies weather patterns. For questions 24 to 30, choose the best answer: A, B or C.

Interviewer   Today's guest is the climate scientist and presenter of the highly entertaining podcast 'Science Stories', Dr Mark Richards. Welcome!

Speaker   Thank you! Actually, I think I'm basically known as 'that scientist who's always talking about clouds!'

Interviewer   And do you usually get a positive reaction when you mention your work to new people?

Speaker   Generally, yes! I mean, I keep it quite simple so it's easy to follow. But actually, people are often amazed when they find out how vital it is to study clouds. And that's when I encourage them to take part in our research.

Interviewer   We'll talk more about your latest research in a moment. But what is it about clouds in particular that interests you?

Speaker   Well, during my studies, I'd done some research on oceans and weather patterns. These areas are probably more well-known when it comes to climate science, and they're certainly fascinating. But since then, I've realised that there's still so much we need to discover about clouds. That's so motivating to me as a scientist.

Interviewer   So, can you give some examples of the types of things you research in your work?

Speaker   Well, clouds can both cool down and also heat up the planet, so they play an important role in understanding climate. And of course, they protect us from strong sunlight. So, we need to understand why they vary so much in terms of their shape and size. That's what I'm currently studying. And this research has taken me to many interesting locations.

Interviewer   And you mentioned that you're keen for people to get involved in your research. This is quite a common thing nowadays, isn't it? I mean, for the general public to contribute to scientific research.

Speaker   Yes, I definitely support citizen science projects.

Interviewer   Well, I imagine it helps you complete your work sooner!

Speaker   Not necessarily! These projects often highlight things we hadn't originally considered, so it can actually be the opposite! But they're perfect when we need to collect statistics and information on a very large scale.

Interviewer   So, at the moment you're asking people to record their observations of clouds. But surely using satellite technology would produce more accurate results?

Speaker   Obviously, it's great that universities have the financial resources to invest in satellites. But this equipment is less useful in certain weather conditions, such as snow. And anyway, satellites provide a view of the clouds from above, but I'm currently interested in looking at them from below – I mean, from the ground.

Interviewer   And so many people are keen to help you record the data. But do they need any special scientific qualifications?

Speaker   Not at all! We provide full training, but actually, what we ask our volunteers to do is really simple. And there isn't a long-term commitment either. Most people send in data

Cambridge B2 First Listening

Interviewer	just a few times, and that's fine. But it's great to see that we have so many volunteers. The vast majority are people with a keen interest in climate issues like global warming, and this is a simple way for them to do their bit.

Interviewer And then there's your podcast too! Is it difficult to balance your academic work with your broadcasting role?

Speaker I think they complement each other. The podcast allows me to spread the word about my research. But, more than that, it helps people discover an interest in science for the first time, and nothing beats that! But what's surprised me so much is that I've learnt just as much from the audience, which is fantastic. They really know their stuff!

Interviewer Well, that's great, Mark. And good luck with all your projects!

Test 6

Part 1
Audio track: B2_Listening_6_1.mp3

Part 1. You will hear people talking in eight different situations. For questions 1 to 8, you must choose the best answer: A, B or C.

Question 1 **You hear two people talking about a job interview. Why is the man disappointed?**

Speaker 1 How did the interview go? Do you think you've got it?

Speaker 2 I don't know. I mean, they seemed quite impressed with what I was saying, I suppose.

Speaker 1 You don't sound very convinced. I know how well you prepared for the presentation – I'm sure you were fantastic.

Speaker 2 Oh, well they told me that they were running late so they didn't ask me to do it. It was all quite disorganised.

Speaker 1 Oh dear!

Speaker 2 To be honest, what they told about the job itself didn't sound very appealing. Not at all what I'd imagined when I applied, so overall, it wasn't a great experience.

Question 2 **You hear a woman on the radio talking about houseplants. What does she think is the main mistake people make with houseplants?**

If you want your houseplants to stay healthy, there are some simple things to keep in mind. Certain plants need very sunny rooms to grow well, whereas others can survive in darker spaces. So, think about that before you choose your houseplants, and choose the right size of plant for your space, too! But, more than anything else, most people go wrong with how they care for their houseplants. They often assume brown leaves means the plant's thirsty, but it's often quite the opposite! Plants can't cope with too much water, so if the beautiful green leaves are going brown, it could be a sign that they are suffering.

Transcripts

Question 3 **You overhear a conversation in a clothes shop. What is the problem?**

Speaker 1 So, with the items you ordered last week and these extra t-shirts, the balance comes to £86.72.

Speaker 2 That doesn't include the skirt, does it? I don't want it anymore because it wasn't the one I meant to order.

Speaker 1 That's right, I've taken that off the total. How would you like to pay?

Speaker 2 Could I put half of it on my credit card and pay for the rest in cash?

Speaker 1 Oh, I'm sorry. I'm afraid we only take debit cards.

Speaker 2 Oh, really? I didn't realise that. I'll have to leave the t-shirts then because I don't have that card on me.

Speaker 1 OK. In that case, that'll be £32.56, please.

Question 4 **You hear two students talking about a lesson they have just had. What did they learn in today's lesson?**

Speaker 1 I'm glad Miss Jones did that session today. The class project's much clearer now.

Speaker 2 Definitely! When she said last week that we'd be writing an 800-word essay and giving a presentation, I panicked!

Speaker 1 Yes, but after today's lesson, as least we know how to collect all the articles and data. It doesn't look as hard as I'd imagined.

Speaker 2 Especially now we can evaluate a source to decide if it's worth using.

Speaker 1 That's going to be the key with the controversial topic I've chosen.

Speaker 2 Oh, wow, you're ahead of me – I haven't picked my subject yet!

Question 5 **You hear a man talking to his friend about a gift he has received. How does he feel about the gift?**

Speaker 1 Is it true your boss presented you with a watch today?

Speaker 2 Yes, it was a 'thank-you' gift for completing that project I told you about. You remember? The one that was a complete nightmare.

Speaker 1 Well, you can always give it to me if you don't like it. I'd happily wear it!

Speaker 2 Well, no, that would cause more problems. But I'm pretty anxious about the whole thing. Why did they choose a watch? Do you think it was a joke about time management? I know I was late a few times but…

Speaker 1 No, you're thinking too deeply about it. It was just a nice gift!

Question 6 **You hear a woman leaving a voicemail for her classmate. What is the woman doing?**

Hi Mark, I'm sorry you couldn't join us to work on the group presentation. I showed the others the PowerPoint we've been working on. Anna doesn't think the pictures will look very clear when we show them on the big screen, and she's right. Rob recommended using a blue background instead. I'm not sure if that'll work, but let's try and then he can tell us if he thinks that's better. The good news is that everyone liked the content. But if you remember Carol's presentation yesterday, it was much shorter,

Cambridge B2 First Listening

so the general feeling was that we'll need to cut some stuff.

Question 7   **You overhear two friends talking about a wedding. What do they agree on?**

Speaker 1   Did you enjoy Harry and Ella's wedding party? I barely got a chance to talk to you when I was there!

Speaker 2   I know, I've never seen such a big crowd of people! But that made it fun.

Speaker 1   Not when you're waiting for the food to be served! But it was a really romantic place to get married, I thought. The gardens were lovely and the dancefloor was so beautiful. It was like a Hollywood film!

Speaker 2   Definitely, they couldn't have picked a better place. But talking about the dancefloor, I wasn't very keen on the band they hired. They played some really strange songs.

Speaker 1   I didn't really notice to be honest – I was too busy dancing!

Question 8   **You hear a man leaving a voicemail message. What is he talking about?**

Hi Lucy, it's Dad. I'm still coming to pick you up but the traffic's really bad today because there are some road closures in the city centre. I think it'll take too long for me to come and collect you from the train station, but what I can do is wait for you at the shopping centre car park instead. That way I won't need to drive through the town centre. So I'll see you there, OK?

Part 2

Audio track: B2_Listening_6_2.mp3

Part 2. You hear Dr Olivia Freeman, an education expert, talking about children's playgrounds. For questions 9 to 18, complete the sentences with a word or short phrase.

In my role as an education expert, I investigate many different aspects of children's development. One field of study I'm particularly interested in is children's playgrounds and play areas. Originally, I began by studying how play areas can affect children's social skills. And what I discovered in this initial research convinced me that playgrounds are vital.

I identified a direct link between playgrounds and children learning to share and help others. In fact, in my study, it became clear that the children that spent more time outside in play areas or playgrounds were less selfish. For instance, they were more willing to take turns in activities. And interestingly, this behaviour continued in the way they behaved during classes too.

Now, this ability to share and interact with others is obviously hugely beneficial because these are skills that will help children throughout their lives. However, above all, I noticed that children who are able to access playgrounds have increased confidence. This seems to be the main benefit for children in terms of their social development.

And of course, it's also important to get the views of the people who teach children to find out what they think about playgrounds. Many teachers or classroom assistants believe that it is essential for children to have opportunities to play outside. They report that playgrounds encourage children to be more creative with their play. And it seems that this can have positive effects on their learning in the classroom too.

But my research didn't end there. I continued with a second study to look at other aspects of playgrounds. And this time I was more focused on playground equipment. So, in this study, I compared and evaluated the physical benefits different types of equipment can offer.

Obviously, all equipment can improve levels of fitness because children balance, jump and swing while using them. These are great ways for children to become fitter and stronger. Most playgrounds include equipment where children move around with their arms in an overhead position. This is important because this movement helps children develop their upper-body strength. I'd particularly suggest monkey bars, because my research showed this was the best piece of equipment for that purpose.

So, my research has shown that playgrounds can bring clear benefits to children. And that's why I now campaign for more opportunities for children to access playgrounds outside school. In my opinion, children living in urban areas have a particular need for these facilities. When they don't have access to fields and the countryside, then playgrounds become even more important.

Of course, designing a playground can involve many complex factors, and obviously there are practical and financial decisions to make. But as an educational expert, I can suggest ways to design playgrounds to make them as beneficial for children as possible. So, I now work as a consultant to help councils plan and design their play areas and playgrounds. It's such an honour to be involved in that.

So, what makes a good playground? Well, as far as I'm concerned, the key thing to think about is variety. I don't mean that playgrounds must all have a wide range of equipment, but they should be designed in a way that encourages children to get involved in different types of play. The possibilities of playground design are endless. But the good news for schools and local authorities is that good playgrounds don't need to be expensive. In fact, I'm definitely in favour of using recycled materials in play areas. This can bring down costs and is better for the environment.

Part 3

Audio track: B2_Listening_6_3.mp3

Part 3. You will hear five short extracts in which people are talking about a common topic. For questions 19 to 23, choose the best answer: A–H. Use the letters only once. There are three extra statements which are not attributed to a speaker.

You hear five people talking about the devices they own.

Speaker 1 I don't mind being called a geek! I love using all sorts of devices in my daily life, and I'm always fascinated to learn about how they work – you know, their operating systems, and how they're put together. I'm always keen to get my hands on the latest device as soon as it's available. I like being ahead of the crowd when it comes to tech trends. Of course, it doesn't always work out that way. I've got so many gadgets that have never really taken off. That makes it difficult to find replacement parts when something goes wrong with them.

Speaker 2 I've also started wearing a smart watch. It's linked to my phone which is pretty handy. I know it can do things like send messages or make calls, but that's not why I bought the watch. I'm trying to be more active and basically be a bit healthier, and the great thing about this watch is that it can monitor my heart rate, how well I'm sleeping and how much exercise I'm doing. Believe it or not, it's really motivating, and I'm definitely making more of an effort to move more now!

Cambridge B2 First Listening

Speaker 3 I don't think I have that many devices. I mean, I've got a laptop which I need for schoolwork, plus a phone of course, but that's it. I was thinking of asking my parents for a games console, but after checking the prices, I realised there's no way I could ask my parents for one. But last year, the local shopping centre was holding some kind of prize draw as part of a special promotion. It was free to enter, and I was absolutely shocked when I won the exact games console that I'd wanted. It's by far the best thing I've ever owned!

Speaker 4 I'm not someone that is really into gadgets or devices for their own sake. For me, they're just things that perform useful functions, rather than beautiful objects. I don't get attached to any of my devices, and when it's time to get a new one I just go for whichever model is affordable and works well. But having said that, I do wish I still had my old digital camera. Even though I've had more expensive models since then, I've never found anything that took shots as well as that one. Sadly, it got smashed to bits when I dropped it on holiday.

Speaker 5 I'm not obsessed with technology, and I can certainly live without most of my devices quite happily. Something that drives me mad about technology is that it's impossible to keep up with all the innovations. That doesn't bother me with things like TVs or computers, but I use my phone all the time so I do want to have the best technology. In fact, I'm thinking of getting a new one. I'm really after one with a bigger and better screen. But it's annoying to know that as soon as I get one, there'll be something else that's even better.

Part 4

Audio track: B2_Listening_6_4.mp3

Part 4. You hear an interview with a university professor called Rachel Sanders, who is talking about history. For questions 24 to 30, choose the best answer: A, B or C.

Interviewer Now, Warbridge University is opening its doors to the public for its History Festival. With us to tell us more is Dr Rachel Sanders. Lovely to have you here, Dr Sanders. So, what's the festival all about?

Speaker Well, our university has an excellent reputation for its international history degrees, but we mustn't forget about all the fascinating history right here in our own neighbourhoods. So, we want to put the spotlight on that and hopefully inspire people to find out more about the stories that have helped to shape Warbridge's identity. And what better week to do that than during the 500th anniversary of Thomas Warbridge's birth?

Interviewer Ah yes, our city's founder! And you'll be sharing the results of your research at the ancient Barton Kirk site.

Speaker That's right. Last year, pottery and other important objects were discovered there – items we believe were used in religious ceremonies. We knew the likely age of these objects, but we weren't sure whether Barton Kirk itself was only used for ceremonies or if it was a residential site. So, my colleagues and I recently returned to investigate that.

Interviewer You must have been terrified of breaking the ancient objects!

Speaker Yes, we handled them extremely carefully! But many artefacts were already damaged when we found them. And many of them had been exposed to harsh sunlight, or rain and snow for years, so we believe their appearance had changed considerably. That's been the biggest challenge for us. We could have easily been misled about Barton Kirk based on these items.

Interviewer So, at the festival, what exactly will you be talking about?

Speaker Well, I'll be discussing ancient ceremonies at Barton Kirk. We know that, as well as

Transcripts

Interviewer	poetry, music played an important role in these ceremonies. We've even found illustrations of the instruments played. And ancient documents provide clues about the type of food that was eaten at these ceremonies too. So, if you'd like to taste some of these dishes, come along to my talk!
Interviewer	What a great way to bring history to life! You're obviously passionate about your work.
Speaker	Oh, definitely, and I've had so many career highlights. The first one was publishing my book, which was a great achievement. I also get a lot of satisfaction from leading my department. But being in the classroom is where I'm happiest. That's given me such pride.
Interviewer	And you've recently been voted Best Educator at Warbridge University.
Speaker	Yes, the greatest honour of my career!
Interviewer	But what would you say to people who think that studying history is a waste of time?
Speaker	Well, you won't be surprised to hear that I disagree. It's not just about looking at ancient texts! There are very real practical uses too, like learning to preserve our historical sites and architecture. And the course I've just started teaching is all about how we can use the latest computer technology in our field of research. But the thing is, the skills learnt in this course can be used for other purposes.
Interviewer	And a lot of people love visiting historical sites, of course, so it brings in a lot of tourism.
Speaker	Yes, and provided it's managed properly, there's no reason why this sector won't develop even further. But I'm still a little cautious – relying on tourism to generate interest in history might not be the answer.
Interviewer	Why's that?
Speaker	I just think the tourism companies tend to focus on entertainment more than historical information. So, speaking from the perspective of a teacher, I just think there are other ways we can promote history.
Interviewer	Well, that's all we have time for, but thanks for joining us Dr Sanders.
Speaker	My pleasure.

How to download the audio

To download the accompanying audio files, please visit our website:

prosperityeducation.net/fce-listening-audio-download-2

Use the password TIAB to access this page.

Click on the book image to download the audio.

The audio file size for all six tests is approximately 180MB.

Leave us a review

By the way, if you enjoy our book, it would be great if you could leave us a review on Amazon. We're a small publisher and every review makes a difference to us and to our lovely team of authors :-)